Serena Anderlini-D'Onofrio
Editor

Women and Bisexuality: A Global Perspective

Women and Bisexuality: A Global Perspective has been co-published simultaneously as *Journal of Bisexuality*, Volume 3, Number 1 2003.

Pre-publication
REVIEWS,
COMMENTARIES,
EVALUATIONS . . .

"Nimbly straddles disciplinary and geographical boundaries. . . . The collection's diversity of subject matter and theoretical perspectives offers a useful model for the continued development of interdisciplinary sexuality studies."

Maria Pramaggiore, PhD
Associate Professor of Film Studies
North Carolina State University

Women and Bisexuality: A Global Perspective

Women and Bisexuality: A Global Perspective has been co-published simultaneously as *Journal of Bisexuality*, Volume 3, Number 1 2003.

The *Journal of Bisexuality* Monographic "Separates"

Below is a list of "separates," which in serials librarianship means a special issue simultaneously published as a special journal issue or double-issue *and* as a "separate" hardbound monograph. (This is a format which we also call a "DocuSerial.")

"Separates" are published because specialized libraries or professionals may wish to purchase a specific thematic issue by itself in a format which can be separately cataloged and shelved, as opposed to purchasing the journal on an on-going basis. Faculty members may also more easily consider a "separate" for classroom adoption.

"Separates" are carefully classified separately with the major book jobbers so that the journal tie-in can be noted on new book order slips to avoid duplicate purchasing.

You may wish to visit Haworth's website at . . .

http://www.HaworthPress.com

. . . to search our online catalog for complete tables of contents of these separates and related publications.

You may also call 1-800-HAWORTH (outside US/Canada: 607-722-5857), or Fax: 1-800-895-0582 (outside US/Canada: 607-771-0012), or e-mail at:

docdelivery@haworthpress.com

Women and Bisexuality: A Global Perspective, edited by Serena Anderlini-D'Onofrio, PhD (Vol. 3, No. 1, 2003). *"Nimbly straddles disciplinary and geographical boundaries. . . . The collection's diversity of subject matter and theoretical perspectives offers a useful model for the continued development of interdisciplinary sexuality studies." (Maria Pramaggiore, PhD, Associate Professor of Film Studies, North Carolina State University)*

Bisexual Women in the Twenty-First Century, edited by Dawn Atkins, PhD (cand.) (Vol. 2, Nos. 2/3, 2002). *An eclectic collection of articles that typifies an ongoing feminist process of theory grounded in life experience.*

Bisexual Men in Culture and Society, edited by Brett Beemyn, PhD, and Erich Steinman, PhD (cand.) (Vol. 2, No. 1, 2002). *Incisive examinations of the cultural meanings of bisexuality, including the overlooked bisexual themes in James Baldwin's classic novels* Another Country *and* Giovanni's Room, *the conflicts within sexual-identity politics between gay men and bisexual men, and the recurring figure of the predatory, immoral bisexual man in novels, films, and women's magazines.*

Bisexuality in the Lives of Men: Facts and Fictions, edited by Brett Beemyn, PhD, and Erich Steinman, PhD (cand.) (Vol. 1, Nos. 2/3, 2001). *"At last, a source book which explains bisexual male desires, practices, and identities in a language all of us can understand! This is informative reading for a general audience, and will be especially valuable for discussions in gender studies, sexuality studies, and men's studies courses." (William L. Leap, PhD, Professor, Department of Anthropology, American University, Washington, DC)*

Women and Bisexuality: A Global Perspective

Serena Anderlini-D'Onofrio, PhD
Editor

Women and Bisexuality: A Global Perspective has been co-published simultaneously as *Journal of Bisexuality*, Volume 3, Number 1 2003.

Harrington Park Press
An Imprint of
The Haworth Press, Inc.
New York • London • Oxford

Published by

Harrington Park Press®, 10 Alice Street, Binghamton, NY 13904-1580 USA

Harrington Park Press is an imprint of The Haworth Press, Inc., 10 Alice Street, Binghamton, NY 13904-1580 USA

Women and Bisexuality: A Global Perspective has been co-published simultaneously as *Journal of Bisexuality*, Volume 3, Number 1 2003.

The development, preparation, and publication of this work has been undertaken with great care. However, the publisher, employees, editors, and agents of The Haworth Press and all imprints of The Haworth Press, Inc., including The Haworth Medical Press® and Pharmaceutical Products Press®, are not responsible for any errors contained herein or for consequences that may ensue from use of materials or information contained in this work. Opinions expressed by the author(s) are not necessarily those of The Haworth Press, Inc. With regard to case studies, identities and circumstances of individuals discussed herein have been changed to protect confidentiality. Any resemblance to actual persons, living or dead, is entirely coincidental.

Cover design by Brooke R. Stiles

Library of Congress Cataloging-in-Publication Data

Anderlini-D'Onofrio, Serena, 1954-
Women and bisexuality: a global perspective / Serena Anderlini-d'Onofrio.
    p. cm.
    "Co-published silmultaneously as Journal of bisexuality, volume 3, number 1, 2003."
    Includes bibliographical references.
    ISBN 1-56023-270-6 (case : alk. paper) – ISBN 1-56023-271-4 (soft : alk. paper)
    1. Bisexuality. 2. Bisexual women–Psychology. I. Journal of bisexuality. II. Title.
HQ74.A53 2003
306.76'5–dc21
                                                                              2003002275

Indexing, Abstracting & Website/Internet Coverage

This section provides you with a list of major indexing & abstracting services. That is to say, each service began covering this periodical during the year noted in the right column. Most Websites which are listed below have indicated that they will either post, disseminate, compile, archive, cite or alert their own Website users with research-based content from this work. (This list is as current as the copyright date of this publication.)

Abstracting, Website/Indexing Coverage . . . . Year When Coverage Began

- *Abstracts in Anthropology* **2000**

- *Book Review Index* **2000**

- *CNPIEC Reference Guide: Chinese National Directory*
  of Foreign Periodicals **2000**

- *e-psyche, LLC <www.e-psyche.net>* **2001**

- *Gay & Lesbian Abstracts <www.nisc.com>* **2000**

- *HOMODOK/"Relevant" Bibliographic Database,*
  Documentation Centre for Gay & Lesbian Studies,
  University of Amsterdam **2000**

- *IBZ International Bibliography of Periodical Literature*
  <www.saur.de> **2002**

- *Index to Periodical Articles Related to Law* **2000**

- *Journal of Social Work Practice "Abstracts Section"*
  <www.carfax.co.uk/jsw-ad.htm> **2000**

(continued)

*Special Bibliographic Notes related to special journal issues
(separates) and indexing/abstracting:*

- indexing/abstracting services in this list will also cover material in any "separate" that is co-published simultaneously with Haworth's special thematic journal issue or DocuSerial. Indexing/abstracting usually covers material at the article/chapter level.
- monographic co-editions are intended for either non-subscribers or libraries which intend to purchase a second copy for their circulating collections.
- monographic co-editions are reported to all jobbers/wholesalers/approval plans. The source journal is listed as the "series" to assist the prevention of duplicate purchasing in the same manner utilized for books-in-series.
- to facilitate user/access services all indexing/abstracting services are encouraged to utilize the co-indexing entry note indicated at the bottom of the first page of each article/chapter/contribution.
- this is intended to assist a library user of any reference tool (whether print, electronic, online, or CD-ROM) to locate the monographic version if the library has purchased this version but not a subscription to the source journal.
- individual articles/chapters in any Haworth publication are also available through the Haworth Document Delivery Service (HDDS).

Women and Bisexuality:
A Global Perspective

CONTENTS

ABOUT THE EDITOR

Serena Anderlini-D'Onofrio, PhD, is Associate Professor in the Department of Humanities at the University of Puerto Rico at Mayaguez. She is the author of *The "Weak" Subject: On Modernity, Eros, and Women's Playwriting* (Associated University Presses, 1998), a comparative theory of women's erotic desires and contributions to modern drama. Her numerous articles on women's writing and relatedness have appeared in several refereed journals. Between 1995 and 1997, she co-coordinated the Bisexual Forum of San Diego. Her most recent article, "Grammars of Touch: Physical, Spiritual, and Erotic Bodies in Massage Therapy," has appeared in *Consciousness, Literature, and the Arts* (April 2002). She is currently working on a memoir and on a book on bisexuality, health, feminism, ecology, and holism.

About the Contributors

Jo Eadie is a European activist and academic based in England. He helped to set up the UK's national bisexual newsletter, *Bi Community News*, co-edited *The Bisexual Imaginary*, and has contributed papers on bisexuality to *Activating Theory* and *Bisexual Men in Culture and Society*. He is currently ill with chronic fatigue syndrome, from which he hopes he will recover one day soon (E-mail: jpe1@staff.ac.uk).

Ingrid R. Ehrbar, MA, is a doctoral student at the Illinois School of Professional Psychology, Chicago Campus. She is very interested in sex, gender, sexuality, and diversity issues in general. Other interests include sex, gender, and sexuality, and issues of couples and families. Correspondence concerning her poem should be addressed to Ingrid R. Ehrbar, Illinois School of Professional Psychology/Chicago Campus, Two First National Plaza, 20 South Clark Street, Third Floor, Chicago, Illinois 60603 (E-mail: IREhrbar@att.net).

Sara Lubowitz is a researcher, writer and activist in HIV/sexual health education and support. Her work includes establishing the Women Partners of Bisexual Men Project at the AIDS Council of New South Wales, Australia, which involved the facilitation of peer support groups and the production/publication of educational materials, such as booklets, posters and video training programs (E-mail: mariapc@deakin.edu.au).

Heather E. Macalister, PhD, is a psychologist specializing in adult development and psychology of women. She currently works at Duke University (E-mail: hmacalister@nc.rr.com).

Maria Pallotta-Chiarolli is a Senior Lecturer in the School of Health Sciences, Deakin University, Melbourne, Australia. She has published several books, chapters, and articles on issues of gender, sexuality, and ethnicity in health and education. These include *Someone You Know* (Wakefield Press, 1991, 2002), Australia's first AIDS biography; *Girls' Talk*: *Young Women Speak Their Hearts and Minds* (Finch Publishing, 1998); *Tapestry: Five*

Generations in an Italian Family (Random House, 1999); and *Boys' Stuff: Boys Talking About What Matters* (co-authored with Wayne Martino, Allen & Unwin, 2001). Maria welcomes information for, and participation in, her current research into the schooling experiences of bisexual people and children from multipartnered and multisexual families, for her forthcoming book, *Border Sexualities and Border Families in Education* (Rowman & Littlefield, 2004) (E-mail: mariapc@deakin.edu.au).

Regina Reinhardt has a PhD in Counseling Psychology and was in private practice for 12 years in San Diego. She is on the Board of Directors of the American Institute of Bisexuality and the Bisexual Forum, a support and discussion group for bisexuals, and was on the steering committee for the 1993 and 1998 Bi-West Conferences. She has given lectures on bisexual relationships at different forums, including at the International Bisexual Conference in Berlin, Germany and Rotterdam, The Netherlands, and has appeared on local television. She organized the first ever Bisexual Art Exhibit in San Diego and she sculpts human figures depicting a bisexual motif. She is the Assistant to the Editor of the *Journal of Bisexuality.*

Heidi Reyes is a fiberartist and poet. Her fiberart includes weaving on a floor loom, an inkle loom and on a tapestry loom, and crocheting. Most of her fiberart, as well as her painting and drawing, reflects her Mexican heritage. The other elements of her fiberart, painting, and drawing reflect her American heritage as she has lived and experienced it in the midwest. She also enjoys expressing herself through written poetry. Some of her poetry reflects her Mexican heritage and some reflects her American heritage, demonstrating her bicultural understanding of her life.

Cheryl Stobie is a lecturer in English and Gender Studies at the University of Natal, Pietermaritzburg, South Africa. She is particularly interested in disruptions of codified binaries. Her recent research has been on sheela-na-gigs, the portrayal of sexuality in contemporary South African novels, and drag kings (E-mail: StobieC@nu.ac.za).

Jennifer Taub is currently completing a postdoctoral fellowship in Clinical Psychology at the Children's Hospital and Harvard Medical School, in Boston, MA. Her various research interests include bisexuality, children's mental health services, and program evaluation. In September 2002, she will join the faculty of the Center for Mental Health Services Research at the University of Massachusetts Medical School, where she will be evaluating children's Medicaid-funded mental health programs.

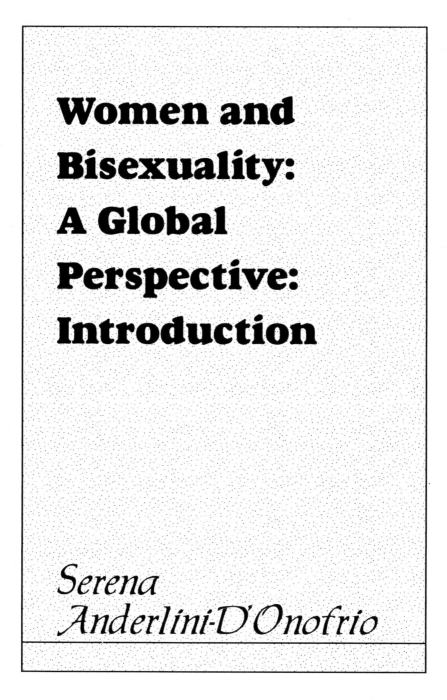

Women and Bisexuality: A Global Perspective: Introduction

Serena Anderlini-D'Onofrio

[Haworth co-indexing entry note]: "Women and Bisexuality: A Global Perspective: Introduction."
Anderlini-D'Onofrio, Serena. Co-published simultaneously in *Journal of Bisexuality* (Harrington Park Press,
an imprint of The Haworth Press, Inc.) Vol. 3, No. 1, 2003, pp. 1-8; and: *Women and Bisexuality: A Global
Perspective* (ed: Serena Anderlini-D'Onofrio) Harrington Park Press, an imprint of The Haworth Press, Inc.,
2003, pp. 1-8. Single or multiple copies of this article are available for a fee from The Haworth Document Delivery Service [1-800-HAWORTH, 9:00 a.m. - 5:00 p.m. (EST). E-mail address: docdelivery@
haworthpress.com].

In the late 1990s, I moved from San Diego, California, to Western Puerto Rico, in the Caribbean, for a job. In San Diego I had my roots in the local bisexual community and had participated in the bisexual movement. I was afraid that the move was going to cut me off from these important parts of my life. I have now been in Puerto Rico for five years, back on my academic career track. What I feared has not happened, quite the opposite. I am out as bi to my friends and colleagues, I give talks about bisexuality at the research colloquium on my campus, and I even get called for advice about multiple-partner relationships. Editing this volume has helped me understand why.

In the 1990s bisexuality was a movement that grew out of the uncomfortable position bi's came to occupy in the gay and lesbian liberation movement, whose focus on identity politics had become somewhat narrow. The AIDS scare only made the position of bi men more awkward, since they were often blamed for being promiscuous, and, therefore, spreading infections. Bi's were the "fence sitters" and the "cop-outs" who wanted the benefits of gay liberation but were not prepared to participate in its struggles. Bi women did not suffer from the same stigma. At this time, most bi women activists had formed themselves in the feminist movement. They were expert collaborators, communicators, and organizers. As feminists, these leaders articulated a position that countered the negative stereotyping. Their sense of community and equality gave bisexuality a forthright, inclusive character. Women were its ideological protagonists and they were also at the forefront in the safer-sex education campaigns that made sex-positive standpoints possible in those difficult times.

By and large, bisexuals contributed to queer cultural discourse a fluid and hybrid sense of identity and an influx notion of sexual orientation that takes into account genetic and environmental factors, as well as individual and group choices. According to bisexual theorist Merl Storr, a binary construction of sexual orientation has so far prevailed in the "hyperdeveloped" world, namely in affluent, high tech, and industrialized societies. This binarism, which constructed homosexual and heterosexual eroticism as incompatible, had often too readily been accepted by gay and lesbian cultures, sometimes as a bargain for acceptance by the larger society. In the 1990s, bisexuals shook up the ground on which this binary construction rested, to point to the reality of bisexual experiences and practices, both within and outside of gay communities, and to the need to develop a thought that would reflect this reality. By necessity, this movement was localized in the urban and metropolitan areas that in the 1980s had been the centers of gay culture. Yet its hybridity made it especially hospitable to transnational and transcultural people, while a sense of global ecology was implied in the naturism of many of its participants. Therein the kernel of its potential for expanding and multiplying.

Not surprisingly, therefore, in this beginning of the third millennium, bisexuality has gone global. That is to say that, just like me, it has traveled from these centers to more peripheral areas, so that at this time hardly any continent has not been touched by it. The authors included in this volume are based in four different continents, including America, Europe, Australia, and Africa, and, more specifically, in the regions of England, New England, California, The Caribbean, and South Africa. The areas in which the situations of bi women are analyzed include France, North America, Germany, Australia, and Sub-Saharan Africa, with historical times in focus ranging from World War II to the present. The need to forge a language that reflects the reality of bisexuality and the situatedness of women in it resonates across the collection.

Significantly, the essays also map the inroads made by bisexual studies into conventional disciplines. In the 1960s, a traditional focus on psychoanalysis prevailed, with its preoccupation with measuring sexual orientation and resolving Oedipal patterns. The scope of the inquiry has now expanded to disciplines, including anthropology, sociology, health, literature, film, history, and biography. As with all knowledge designed to challenge set categories, in bisexual studies, interdisciplinarity is not just politically correct. It is absolutely necessary. Rather than following prescribed models, authors design their own patterns based on their genuine empirical observation. Approaches in use include critical theory, deconstruction, textual analysis, cognitive psychology, the personal essay, the review essay, reportage, qualitative study, and all combinations thereof necessary to adhere to the diverse bisexual realities under investigation. Since bisexuality challenges the categories according to which eroticism is constructed, deconstruction is a theoretical point of reference. Theorists like Jacques Derrida, Michel Foucault, Gilles Deleuze, and Julia Kristeva have blazed the path for a thought deconstructive of sexual binarisms. Accordingly, they are referred to by several authors. Also referred to are others who have followed in their path are Trihn T. Minh-ha, Gloria Anzaldua, and Elaine Showalter. From the collection, bisexuality comes across as a discursive space located at the interstice between gay and straight cultures that can function as a bridge between postindustrial and neocolonial societies. Its eroticism is a hybrid of premodern and postmodern sexualities as they coexist in today's world.

Jennifer Taub uses the questionnaire, a conventional tool of sociological inquiry, to analyze the impact of women's communities and feminism on bi women's appearance and sense of their bodies. The author explains that open questions led to qualitative analysis based on recurrent themes in samples. The procedure is empirical rather than model-based, hence truer to the reality under investigation and more incisive. Taub found out that feminism and contact with women's communities made bi women more capable of accepting their own physical self, and of defining their own aesthetic standards, independently of media stereotypes. Some women stopped beauty practices that caused useless suffering. Some adopted "dyke looks" and learned to value themselves for who they were rather than for their appearance. Others learned to appreciate the beauty and abundance of women of size.

Heather Macalister uses a combination of personal essay and cognitive analysis to focus on the resistance to categorization that characterizes bisexuality and its effects in her communication with her rather open-minded, but category-dependent, father, who asks her the embarrassing question, "Are there really such things as bisexuals?" The essay points to people's need to categorize observed objects through cognitive schema, which ironically can prevent observers from genuinely seeing what is in front of them. The author wonders what a cognitive schema for a bisexual would look like, since bisexuals include people for whom the gender of the desired object is essential (and, therefore, must have both), and people for whom it is irrelevant (and, therefore, can have either). Macalister confesses that she is not ready to answer her father's question with a simple, "yes, dad, there are and your daughter is one." She vows to send him her essay instead. Her writing springs out of this urge to communicate what has no language yet. One is encouraged to look at the empirical reality behind cognitive categories, and to observe the process through which new realities come into being and coalesce as thought that in turn forms new categories.

Cheryl Stobie summarizes the situation of queer people in Southern Africa, where several postcolonial governments have declared homosexuality an "abominable Western import" and "Un-African." Post-Apartheid South Africa, which in that region has declared itself a "rainbow nation," has become a leader for change, and a shelter for persecuted people in the surrounding countries. In this context, Stobie claims, homophobic campaigns are designed to distract the public from more serious issues like poverty and poor health. Marriage is considered a social obligation, and rape is sometimes practiced as a "cure" for lesbianism. The article proceeds to analyze the content and context of a recent study of queer African sexualities that proves the existence of queer Africans well before colonial times, but does not categorize bisexual behavior as such. Clearly, as Stobie points out, *Boy-wives and Female Husbands: South African Homosexualities*, is a good beginning that begs the question of how behavior can better dovetail with the categories used to describe it. Stobie points to the only essay on women in the book, which describes the erotic aspects of relationships between co-wives in polygamous marriages, a good example of bisexual behavior whose agents are unfortunately not in a position to claim bisexual identity.

Maria Pallotta-Chiarolli and Sara Lubowitz present a series of interviews with Australian bi and/or straight women of diverse cultural and class background, whose primary partners are bisexual men. The interviews are framed by theoretical analyses based on deconstructive categories that demonstrate how these women consciously negotiate their situatedness, including their roles in their relationships, their place in the queer communities of which their couple is part, their couple's place in the ethnic communities its members come from, and their personal spaces separate from their partners. These subjects, the authors argue, are positioned as "outside belonging," namely participants in both their traditional ethnic communities where they pass as straight, and in their queer communities, where their oddity is not quite categorized. Yet, their presence erodes from within the heteronormativity of straight society and the homonormativity of gay society. To these women, the decision to enable their partners' bisexual behavior is empowering, for it is a conscious choice rather than a passive denial. As a result, the women are happier and more self-reliant.

In my own article, I use psychological and textual analysis, archival and biographical research, as well as my theory of labial mimesis and the two-in-one to study the two feminist staples in the career of playwright and memoirist Lillian Hellman. I argue that the bisexual triangles in her 1934 Broadway success *The Children's Hour*, and in the short story "Julia" (1973), later made in to a film, correspond to the patterns of her repressed bisexual fantasies. Also discussed are Hellman's emotional intimacy with her female translators from Russia, and her aura as a writer, with responses from female fans attesting to the impact of her works on their lives. In both stories, a labial duo made of two interdependent female characters occupies center stage. The friendship between the two women is central to their lives and based on an undertow of repressed bisexual erotic impulses. This trope appears at the beginning of the author's career, and reappears in her later life, when she was intent in better understanding the nature of women's friendships and of her own sexual desires. At this time, while she was also reaching out for her roots as a descendent of Jews from Germany, she came to see the compulsory heterosexuality that dominated her youth as a form of erotic totalitarianism. I argue that Hellman's internalized biphobia and her repressed bisexuality are the "ounce of truth" that made her heterosexual identity a lie. They are also the psychological basis for her position as a realist writer.

Ingrid Ehrbar's poem "Fucking Categories," and Heidi Reyes' "The Other" pinpoint two themes that run through this collection, bisexuality's ability to disrupt categories, and the resulting feeling of alienation many bisexuals experience.

Regina Reinhardt's review of a German film about two women in Berlin who fell in love during Nazism, with one being Jewish, points to ways in which bisexual behavior persists under the least favorable circumstances. The film is a German production of the late 1990s. From a true story, it opens a view on the experience of women who loved other women in Nazi Germany, when women who gave birth to sons were awarded special prizes, and when hiding a Jew could cost one's life. The very existence of this film points to how different things are now, at least in liberal-progressive societies.

Finally, Jo Eadie's review essay of a new study of Simone de Beauvoir points to the benefits of reassessing the French philosopher's work in the light of her bisexuality, and to the risks implied in constructing a bisexual canon. The book under review, *Identity without Selfhood: Simone de Beauvoir and Bisexuality*, by Mariam Fraser, discusses the reasons why the issue of bisexuality has been eschewed in previous studies, and suggests ways to use the philosopher's history of bisexual behavior to better understand her work and life. Eadie argues that while it is important to give this behavior its proper name, constructing a bisexual identity for de Beauvoir might be a step in the direction of making bisexuality more tame and categorizable than it has been so far. Eadie also situates Fraser's book within the context of bisexual discourse, pointing out to the different implications of constructing de Beauvoir's bisexual identity for its scholarly and activist developments. If bisexuality is to be a movement based in politics and activism, then constructing a bisexual canon may divert energies from more important goals. Yet, this reassessment of de Beauvoir opens new vistas on the possible discipline of bisexual studies.

At the crossroads between its activist and academic paths, bisexuality is certainly a lively area of knowledge at this time. As this collection indicates, the idea of bisexuality is being employed productively to rethink a number of issues and situations, and this is happening pervasively across the planet. As Merl Storr has suggested, neither does bisexuality need to be a mere identity nor a mere practice. It can be located instead in the interstice between identity and practice where new epistemologies are formed. As an epistemology, bisexuality enables new ways of thinking about experience whose diversity is exemplified in this collection. Its interdisciplinary character makes it even more productive at the turn of a new millennium, in which women's perspectives and modes of knowledge are likely to be valued, and in which new ways of thinking about eroticism, interrelatedness, and coexistence will have to be found.

WORK CITED

Storr, Merl. "Introduction." *Bisexuality: A Critical Reader.* London: Routledge, 1999.

What Should I Wear?

A Qualitative Look at the Impact of Feminism and Women's Communities on Bisexual Women's Appearance

Jennifer Taub

http://www.haworthpress.com/store/product.asp?sku=J159
10.1300/J159v03n01_02

[Haworth co-indexing entry note]: "What Should I Wear? A Qualitative Look at the Impact of Feminism and Women's Communities on Bisexual Women's Appearance." Taub, Jennifer. Co-published simultaneously in *Journal of Bisexuality* (Harrington Park Press, an imprint of The Haworth Press, Inc.) Vol. 3, No. 1, 2003, pp. 9-22; and: *Women and Bisexuality: A Global Perspective* (ed: Serena Anderlini-D'Onofrio) Harrington Park Press, an imprint of The Haworth Press, Inc., 2003, pp. 9-22. Single or multiple copies of this article are available for a fee from The Haworth Document Delivery Service [1-800-HAWORTH, 9:00 a.m. - 5:00 p.m. (EST). E-mail address: docdelivery@haworthpress.com].

SUMMARY. This article examines the effects of feminism and exposure to bisexual lesbian and women's communities on bisexual women's behavior, thoughts and feelings regarding beauty and appearance norms. Seventy-seven bisexual women participated in a qualitative survey addressing these issues. Sixty-two women responded to questions about the ways in which feminism has affected their beauty ideas and/or practices. Results showed that 73% (n = 45) of these respondents felt that feminism affected their beauty ideas and/or practices, with all but one woman citing positive influences. Seventy-six women responded to questions about the ways in which contact with women's communities affected their beauty ideas and/or practices. Results showed that 59% (n = 45) of these respondents felt that contact with women's communities has had an impact on their beauty ideas and/or practices. The majority of respondents (91%; n = 69) also felt that there are clear appearance norms or standards in women's communities that differ from those of society at large. Themes from open-ended responses, specific examples and implications of findings are discussed. *[Article copies available for a fee from The Haworth Document Delivery Service: 1-800-HAWORTH. E-mail address: <docdelivery@haworthpress.com> Website: <http://www.HaworthPress. com> © 2003 by The Haworth Press, Inc. All rights reserved.]*

KEYWORDS. Bisexuality, women, feminism, communities, appearance, beauty, qualitative research

Virtually no attention has been paid to the ways in which appearance expectations of the dominant culture impact bisexual women. The beauty standard for women, seemingly a heterosexual one, is thin and stereotypically feminine. It has been hypothesized that lesbians may find standard appearance norms less important (Rothblum, 1994), presumably because one of the primary reasons women seek to attain such ideals is to attract heterosexual mates. Conversely, it may be that a lesbian beauty standard exists, and that lesbian women may be more likely to seek to attain this standard in order to attract same gender mates.

Four studies have been conducted that have specifically examined differences between lesbians' and heterosexual women's satisfaction with their physical appearance. Three of these four studies found no differences between lesbian and heterosexual women on measures of body dissatisfaction (Beren, Hayden, Wilfley & Grilo, 1996; Brand, Rothblum & Solomon, 1992; Striegel-Moore, Tucker & Hsu, 1990). This research indicated that gender is a more salient feature than sexual orientation regarding appearance concerns such as body weight, yet lesbians still endorsed fewer body image concerns than heterosexual women (Brand, Rothblum & Solomon, 1992). The fourth study found lesbians indicated significantly more body satisfaction than heterosexual women, at the same or heavier body weights (Herzog, Newman, Yeh & Warshaw, 1992). Other research (see Myers, Taub, Morris & Rothblum, 1998) has shown that lesbians perceive greater acceptance of physical appearances not consistent with the dominant culture's norms within lesbian communities. The authors concluded that lesbian beauty norms differ from heterosexual ones.

Feminism appears to be another factor that is related to women's ideas and behavior regarding appearance. One study found a positive correlation between feminist attitudes regarding physical attractiveness and body satisfaction (Dionne, Davis, Fox & Gurevich, 1995). Another study found that women with eating disorders have higher levels of stress related to rigid adherence to traditional feminine gender roles (Martz, Handley & Eisler, 1995). Finally, a third study that looked only at lesbians found that participation in feminist activities was positively correlated with self-acceptance (Leavy & Adams, 1986). The findings of these studies suggest that feminist attitudes and participation in feminist activities are positively related to rejection of traditional appearance norms, and this is also related to overall self-acceptance.

What roles do contact with women's communities have on bisexual women endorsement of such standards? And, if it is true that a distinct lesbian beauty standard exists, are bisexual women more likely to endorse heterosexual or lesbian beauty standards?

Sociologist Paula Rust's (1995) research found that the more heterosexually oriented bisexual women were, the more they preferred to socialize with other bisexuals, while the more homosexually oriented they were, the more they preferred to affiliate with lesbians. Further, bisexual women who were involved in relationships with lesbians were more likely to work for lesbian political concerns and endorse lesbian candidates than were bisexual women who were involved with men. Extrapolating from this research, it would follow that bisexual women who are currently involved with women's communities would adhere more to lesbian beauty standards; bisexual women who have less contact with women's communities, would adhere more to heterosexual appearance norms.

This study was undertaken to examine what roles (1) contact with feminist ideas, and (2) contact with women's communities have on bisexual women's thoughts, feelings and behavior regarding beauty and appearance.

METHODS AND SAMPLE

To answer these questions, 77 bisexual women responded to a written questionnaire through bisexual or GLB mailing lists on the Internet, friendship networks, bisexual organizations, and the snowball technique. The criteria for inclusion were that participants were female, at least 18 years of age, and currently self-identified as bisexual. About 60% of the surveys were returned via e-mail, and the remainders were returned by post.

In response to the question, "What is your racial and/or ethnic identification?" sixty-eight women (88%) identified themselves as white, four (5%) as Asian American, three (4%) as bi- or multiracial, one (1%) as African-American and one (1%) as Latina. Nine women (12%) described themselves as Jewish in addition to white. Participants ranged in age from 18 to 47 (median = 29). The average number of years they had been out as bisexual to themselves was 9.3 years (range 1-29 years), and to others was 7.6 years (range 1-25 years). The mean age at coming out to oneself was 20 and to others was 22.

Fifty-five women (71%) said they were currently partnered or dating, and of these, thirty-two (58%) had a male partner or partners, twenty (36%) had a female partner, and three (5%) had both a male and a female partner.

METHODS OF QUALITATIVE DATA ANALYSIS

Methods for analysis of qualitative data outlined and discussed by Strauss (1987) were used. For each of the questions, open coding, an unrestricted coding procedure to determine categories that fit the data, was first employed by the coder (the author). This was done twice and then axial coding, an intensive coding procedure around each category, was used to identify themes.

RESULTS

Feminism

Sixty-two women responded directly to the following question: How do you feel feminism has affected the role that beauty norms or body image play in your life? Of these women, the majority (76%; N = 47) responded that feminism has had effects on their beauty ideas and/or behavior, and the remaining 24% responded that feminism has had no effect.

Among the forty-six women who reported effects of feminism, seven distinct themes about the ways in which feminism has affected them were identified in their open-ended responses. Women addressed one or more themes in their responses.

1. *Feminism has helped me to develop my own ideas about beauty and appearance.* Over a quarter of this group (13) felt that feminism had been the catalyst in their lives for developing their own beauty ideas. Some of these women spoke about making conscious beauty choices rather than simply accepting and adopting the ones society foists upon women. For example, a 31-year-old said, "Feminism radically changed my perspective on beauty and attractiveness. It has provided a framework for me to realize that beauty is a socially constructed reality. I've realized that 'societal beauty norms' aren't realistically obtainable." And a 37-year-old remarked that to her, feminism is "not what choices I make regarding my beauty practices, but that my choices are conscious and that I am aware of the probable factors involved–that it's a critical process."

2. *Feminism taught me how oppressive societal beauty standards are.* Ten women (22%) spoke about ways in which feminism exposed them to ideas about the oppressiveness of societal appearance dictates for women. For example, a 26-year-old stated, "Feminism has played a central role in how I experience my body by demystifying cultural norms about beauty and body image." And a 37-year-old said, "Feminism made me conscious of the societal pressures on women and their destructive influence on women's self-esteem." These women also spoke about the impact of exposure to feminist theory. For example, a 29-year-old said,

> All of my family members are overweight and I had a lot of shame about it. In college I started accepting my body and feminism helped extremely with that. Feminism helped me crawl out of my preoccupation with weight/image/being heterosexually attractive that I felt as a teenager.

3. *I stopped certain beauty practices because of feminism.* Ten women mentioned concrete behavioral changes they made in their beauty practices as a result of feminism. Women talked about discontinuing practices such as shaving body hair, wearing make-up, wearing uncomfortable clothing or shoes, wearing perfume, or dieting. A 47-year-old said, "When I was growing up I thought women had to wear make up, high heel shoes, bras, girdles, shave legs and armpits. I learned this stuff was all crap, and stopped conforming to it, when I came out as feminist." And a 27-year-old noted,

Becoming feminist has had a bigger impact on my feelings about appearance than anything else has. As I have become feminist I have gone through a period of time when I refused to do many of the stereotypically feminine beauty activities that I used to do, like shaving, wearing make up and perfume, dieting, etc. This was motivated by my awareness of how much time I spend doing all these things (time that would be better spent doing something else), how much energy I was putting into these things that again, could be diverted towards improving my life or the life of other women.

Two of the women addressing this theme also talked about adopting new feminist beauty practices. A 31-year-old said, "Keeping my hair short, wearing ties and sensible shoes are political as well as fashion statements."

4. *Feminism has had a general positive impact.* Ten women (22%) spoke of the effects of feminism in generalized terms. Unlike responses that were coded in the other 6 themes, women who gave responses that were coded in this theme did not address any of the other themes. Women in this group gave responses such as "Feminism has had a positive effect," or spoke of feminists as positive role models in their lives.

5. *I care less about societal beauty norms.* Nine women (20%) felt that feminism resulted in their having less overall concern with, in the words of one woman, "society's opinions" and in the words of another, "heterosexist norms." While a few of these women also talked about developing their own beauty norms, the women who gave responses coded in this theme specifically spoke of devoting less caring, concern or worry to societal beauty standards after their contact with feminism than they had prior to awareness of feminist ideas. For example, a 43-year-old woman said, "I felt more affirmed in feeling that looks were not so important by the feminist movement," while a 23-year-old remarked simply, "[Feminism] makes me less worried about beauty."

6. *Feminism made me more aware of eating disorders.* Finally, three (7%) women spoke specifically of the ways in which feminism had made them more aware of eating disorders. A 19-year-old woman talked about how she had to admit to herself she was anorexic after she read Naomi Wolf's book, *The Beauty Myth*, which she credited with having given her first exposure to feminist ideas about beauty and appearance. And a 27-year-old talked about how her feminism made her question many of the "mainstream beauty activities" she had been engaged in, and said, "I think stopping these things was healthy for me, and prevented me from developing an eating disorder."

7. *Negative effects of feminism.* Three women mentioned what they felt to be negative effects related to feminism on their experiences with beauty and appearance. Only one woman mentioned a negative impact only, without concurrently discussing positive effects of feminism. This 32-year-old woman said, "For a while I bought into the old-style feminist antipathy towards clothing and makeup, then I decided that it was limiting my personal expression." Another woman had concerns that being perceived as a feminist by rejecting societal beauty norms could impact her negatively at work.

Effects of Contact with Bi and Lesbian Communities

Does contact with bi and lesbian communities affect women's beauty or appearance ideas and practices? Participants were asked to discuss their contact with these communities and the importance of this contact in their lives, and on their beauty practices.

Of the seventy-six respondents who answered this question, the overwhelming majority (n = 69; 91%) noted clear differences in appearance in lesbian communities, and, to a lesser extent, bi women's communities, when compared with society at large. While 10% (n = 7) of these women said that these different appearance standards had not affected them personally, the majority of these women (n = 45; 59%) spoke specifically about how these differences in dress, appearance, standards and acceptability in women's communities had affected them personally. There were seven distinct themes identified in the open-ended responses of the forty-six women who reported personal effects. Respondents could address more than one of these themes in their responses, and indeed, more than half of the respondents did so. This next section will focus on the 7 themes that these forty-six women mentioned in discussing the ways in which contact with lesbian, bi or women's communities have personally affected their thoughts, attitudes or behavior regarding beauty and appearance.

1. *Adopting lesbian or "non-traditional" personal/fashion styles.* Just under half (47%; n = 21) of the 46 respondents talked about ways in which they incorporated lesbian beauty norms, "dyke" looks, or "non-traditional" beauty into their own personal styles after having contact with communities in which such styles were observed. They fell into 2 groups.

Dyke looks. Four-fifths of these women spoke specifically of adopting "dyke looks" into their own personal style. Such women seemed to feel that the lesbian standards were ones which felt natural and comfortable to them. One 25-year-old said, "As a bi woman, I feel much freer to look like a dyke because of the lesbian image," a 28-year-old said, "I tend to stick with the dyke standards, and I hate looking femme," and a 30-year-old summed up this sentiment when she remarked, "My short hair, black jeans, colorful vests, etc., are clearly the grad school dyke uniform. Although I identify as a bi woman, I think I've absorbed a lot of my own beauty standards from the lesbian community." Two women also spoke of modeling themselves after the "strong women" they had met in lesbian communities.

In contrast, other women noted that they specifically adopted such a lesbian look when with women's or lesbian communities, essentially adapting to the communities they were with. For example, a 33-year-old said, "When I'm more active in the lesbian community, I tend to dress more unisex, vs. more feminine with the general population," and a 27-year-old expressed this duality when she said, "sometimes I feel like I have two different closets of clothes: my dykey clothes and my het clothes."

Adopting non-traditional looks. Four women talked about ways in which they had adopted new fashions for themselves after exposure to women's communities, but labeled their looks as "non-traditional" or comfortable, rather than specifically lesbian, butch, or bi.

2. *Feeling more freedom/more acceptance to express or be myself appearance-wise.* Nineteen women (42%) noted feeling personally more accepted regardless of what they look like, or feeling more freedom within bi/lesbian/women's communities to express themselves through their appearance. Five women noted feeling this freedom in the bi community, 5 in the lesbian community, and 9 in both communities (or they did not distinguish between them).

Some women talked about feeling more accepted in general, which in turn made them view their own appearance differently. For example, a 23-year-old said, "I feel more beautiful because I feel comfortable [in bi/lesbian communities], and I feel like women don't obsess about other women's bodies as much as men do." A 30-year-old found that both the people and the ideas she came into contact with in her community were transformative for her. She said,

> Discovering women's community and queer community was a huge factor for me in overcoming some of the more destructive implications of beauty norms. I perceived this as a community where I wouldn't be judged for my appearance . . . Contact with the bi community has made me feel so confident about who I am and [how I look].

Other women talked about the power of getting to know women who didn't conform to societal norms and felt comfortable with themselves. A

43-year-old said, "I've grown very close to women who are comfortable with their bodies, which I didn't have before getting involved with a bi community," and a 29-year-old said, "I have met inspirational larger and fat women, which makes me feel welcome and better about myself." Another woman felt that the appearance values she found in the bi community were helpful to her. She said, "The community seems to value strength, not devalue larger or overweight women. No makeup seems to be a norm. As a bi woman, it is affirming and empowering."

3. *Feeling negative personal effects on appearance.* Nineteen women addressed these themes, which fell into 3 subcategories.

a. *Pressures to conform to lesbian standards.* Eight women (42%) noted negative personal effects arising from perceived pressures to conform to lesbian appearance standards. Women spoke of feeling judged if they chose, for example, to shave, or to wear perfume or make-up. For example, a 35-year-old said, "The feeling that being feminine is seen as negative affects the outfit I might wear." A 27-year-old expressed her mixed feelings about feeling such pressures when she said,

> When I go to lesbian events, I sometimes feel pressure to not conform to mainstream beauty standards–to not shave or wear perfume, to not diet, etc. But I also think that women who shave and are skinny, etc., are secretly seen as more attractive. It seems like a double standard–but even a double standard is better that mainstream standards.

Another woman remarked, "I've tended to feel my own need to be 'butchier' when I'm with women–to show I'm one of the crowd."

b. *Too femme.* Six women (32%) felt that they had been unjustly categorized in women's communities as more femme than they felt themselves to be, based on how others perceived their appearance. A 23-year-old expressed her frustration,

> I look at myself as being more butch in personality but in dress I am mostly femme. But then people assume I am femme by how I look and treat me as such, which annoys the hell out of me because I am a hell of a lot stronger than my girlfriend who happens to look like a butch.

And a 43-year-old said,

> In my opinion, there's a lesbian dress code and if you don't adhere to it, acceptance is very unlikely. I don't "look" lesbian. I'm too

"femmy" and it's kept me from being accepted in the lesbian community. . . and it has kept me from being taken seriously as a gay activist.

c. *Don't like bi/lesbian norms.* Finally, five women (26%) expressed their discomfort with bi women's or lesbian norms. For example, a 37-year-old said that she "Felt uncomfortable at the one bi meeting I went to. People were very made up or pierced and I didn't identify with them and walked out."

4. *Having less concern with societal appearance norms.* Eight (18%) women felt that exposure to women's communities resulted in them being simply less concerned in general with beauty or appearance. These women felt that they had become more relaxed about how they looked, and reported feeling more comfortable with themselves. Regarding contact with women's communities, they said things such as: "Made me feel like looks are less important"; "Definitely frees me to define beauty for myself"; and "It made me less self-conscious about my appearance." A 30-year-old found that these communities were "affirming" places where "body image and gender norms do not apply."

5. *Experiencing exposure to feminist ideas about beauty.* Six women (13%) found that exposure to women's communities either introduced them to feminist ideas about beauty, or reinforced those feminist ideas for them. Said one 25-year-old,

> Being in contact with bi and lesbian communities is the same for me as being in contact with feminism in any form, and feminism has definitely opened my eyes to what's going on in our society regarding women and beauty standards and so on.

Another woman remarked,

> My feminism and my bisexuality evolved together, and the two both affected my feelings about beauty. In college it was liberating for me to be around women-identified women who didn't shave their legs or try to be skinny.

6. *Feeling more accepted as a fat woman.* Six women (13%) felt that their weight or size was more accepted within the bi or lesbian communities. (A larger number commented that fat women are viewed more positively in women's communities, but did not address personal impact. However, three of these women also felt that while "fat acceptance" was outwardly expressed, it was not necessarily practiced.)

As noted earlier, women talked about the positive experience of getting to know other women of size who felt comfortable with themselves. A 21-year-old said, "Overweight women are viewed as they once were–as symbols of abundance . . . this has made me more willing to express myself." And a 19-year-old woman discussed her positive experience though a relationship,

> Seems to me that lesbians are heavier, more confident with their weight, maybe because they're not pressured to live up to society's (men's) standards. When I dated a lesbian, she had the same concerns and struggles about body image as I did. I know my relationship with her made me more confident about the weight I'd gained.

7. *Experiencing a change in the role appearance plays in my own attractions to women.* Five women (11%) found their attractions transformed by exposure to women's communities. A 29-year-old said,

> Going to the Michigan Women's Music Festival and seeing all those wonderful naked women was a revelation to me. There were women in all shapes and sizes, colors, ages, and their breasts did not curve up (mostly) but went with gravity like mine. That changed me.

A 25-year-old said,

> I think that as I realized who I found attractive, I began to apply different beauty standards to myself. The realization that I'm not attracted to overly bony women–that I find women's round bodies attractive–made it much easier to look at my own body and love it.

Similarly, a 24-year-old said, "Recognizing my attraction to women, and especially to fat women, was a major factor in overcoming my self-hatred about being a fat woman."

CONCLUSIONS

Results from this study suggest that for women in this sample, both feminism and involvement with women's communities influenced many of their behaviors and attitudes about beauty norms and appearance. Almost three-quarters of the women responding to questions about the influence of feminism on their appearance-related behavior and/or attitudes discussed what they felt to be positive of effects of feminism in their lives. Many of these changes involved a rejection of the dominant culture's norms, and a newfound freedom to create personalized and affirming beauty ideas and practices.

Over ninety percent of the women in this study felt that women's communities, especially lesbian communities, have different appearance norms and standards from society at large. Only a small proportion of these women (10%) said that these norms had not impacted them personally; the majority (59%) discussed specific ways in which they had been affected by the different appearance attitudes and practices that they had encountered in their involvement with women's communities. Many of these women have struggled with not only trying to figure out which communities feel comfortable and accepting to them, but also what they may feel they need to do to gain that acceptance. For many women, this involves a process of altering one's appearance to fit in with what she has observed to be acceptable within each community. Most of these women spoke about the freedom they felt to dress comfortably, to develop their own styles, to feel comfortable with their weight and body image, and to appreciate other women's bodies. However, a large subgroup of these women also felt a new set of pressures, to adopt a new set of standards that didn't feel quite right to them. Further, a number of women felt that they were unjustly stereotyped in these communities as representing societal norms. This was especially frustrating to women who felt that they did not endorse these standards.

Many of these women spoke of adopting their own appearance standards that seem to fall between the stereotypical "feminine" societal norms for women, and the stereotypical lesbian appearance norms. Women talked about having different outfits they wore to different gatherings, or about the ways in which they adopted "soft butch" looks, or integrated traditional and lesbian norms. In keeping with Paula Rust's findings, women who considered themselves to be more lesbian identified or spent time with more lesbian/women's communities spoke proudly of the lesbian looks they adopted. Many women spending time with a bi community spoke more of just feeling comfortable with their appearance, or of having the freedom to develop their own norms. It is clear that, for the women participating in this study, they have been influenced by the non-heterosexual communities that they have become a part of. For many women, this influence extends to the way they present themselves to the world around them, as well as to the ways they feel about their own physical appearance.

Limitations of this study are that this is a self-selected group of women who responded to a survey for bisexual women. Women who may have bisexual behavior but who identify as lesbian or heterosexual are not necessarily represented. Additionally, this sample was primarily Caucasian, and the findings may not extend to women of color, or older women (over age 50).

REFERENCES

Beren, S.E., Hayden, H.A., Wilfley, D.E. & Grilo, C.M. (1996). The influence of sexual orientation on body dissatisfaction in adult men and women. *Int'l Journal of Eating Disorders, 20,* 135-141.

Berscheid, E. & Walster, E. (1984). Physical attractiveness. *Advances in Experimental Social Psychology, 18,* 157-215.

Brand, P.A., Rothblum, E.D. & Solomon, L.J. (1992). A comparison of lesbians, gay men, and heterosexuals on weight and restrained eating. *Int'l Journal of Eating Disorders, 11*(3) 253-259.

Dionne, M., Davis, C., Fox, J. & Gurevich, M. (1995). Feminist ideology as a predictor of body dissatisfaction in women. *Sex Roles, 33*(3-4) 277-287.

Herzog, D.B., Newman, K.L., Yeh, C.J. & Warshaw, M. (1992). Body image satisfaction in homosexual and heterosexual women. *Int'l Journal of Eating Disorders, 11*(4) 391-396.

Leavy, R.L. & Adams, E.M. (1986). Feminism as a correlate of self-esteem, self-acceptance, and social support among lesbians. *Psychology of Women Quarterly, 10*(4) 321-326.

Martz, D.M., Handley, K.B. & Eisler, R.M. (1995). The relationship between feminine gender role stress, body image, and eating disorders. *Psychology of Women Quarterly, 19*(4) 493-508.

Myers, A., Taub, J., Morris, J. & Rothblum, E. (1998). Beauty mandates and the appearance obsession: Are lesbians any better off? In D. Atkins (Ed.), *Looking Queer: Body Image and Identity in Lesbian, Bisexual, Gay and Transgender Communities* (pp. 17-26). New York: The Haworth Press.

Rothblum, E.D. (1994). Lesbians and physical appearance: Which model applies? In B. Greene and G.M. Herek (Eds.), *Psychological Perspectives on Lesbian and Gay Issues, 1,* 84-97.

Rust, P. (1995). *Bisexuality and the Challenge to Lesbian Politics.* New York: New York University Press.

Strauss, A.L. (1987). *Qualitative Analysis for Social Scientists.* Cambridge: Cambridge University Press.

Striegel-Moore, R.H., Tucker, N. & Hsu, J. (1990). Body image dissatisfaction and disordered eating in lesbian college students. *Int'l Journal of Eating Disorders, 9,* 493-500.

Wolf, N. (1991). *The Beauty Myth: How Images of Beauty Are Used Against Women.* New York: William Morrow.

In Defense
of Ambiguity:
Understanding
Bisexuality's
Invisibility Through
Cognitive Psychology

Heather E. Macalister

http://www.haworthpress.com/store/product.asp?sku=J159
© 2003 by The Haworth Press, Inc. All rights reserved.
10.1300/J159v03n01_03

[Haworth co-indexing entry note]: "In Defense of Ambiguity: Understanding Bisexuality's Invisibility Through Cognitive Psychology." Macalister, Heather E. Co-published simultaneously in *Journal of Bisexuality* (Harrington Park Press, an imprint of The Haworth Press, Inc.) Vol. 3, No. 1, 2003, pp. 23-32; and: *Women and Bisexuality: A Global Perspective* (ed: Serena Anderlini-D'Onofrio) Harrington Park Press, an imprint of The Haworth Press, Inc., 2003, pp. 23-32. Single or multiple copies of this article are available for a fee from The Haworth Document Delivery Service [1-800-HAWORTH, 9:00 a.m. - 5:00 p.m. (EST). E-mail address: docdelivery@haworthpress.com].

SUMMARY. Cognitive schema theory is applied to sexual orientation, asserting that humans are most comfortable when sexual orientation can be neatly categorized. Bisexuality is thus cognitively problematic, as it straddles categories and defies markers and stereotypes. Bisexuality and other forms of sexual fluidity may not be accepted as actually existing if they do not fit into people's cognitive schemas, resulting in a denial of bisexuality, bisexuality's invisibility, and a desire to discover the so-called bisexual's "true" sexual orientation. *[Article copies available for a fee from The Haworth Document Delivery Service: 1-800-HAWORTH. E-mail address: <docdelivery@haworthpress.com> Website: <http://www.HaworthPress.com> © 2003 by The Haworth Press, Inc. All rights reserved.]*

KEYWORDS. Bisexuality, cognitive categorization, cognitive schema theory, labeling, schema, sexual fluidity, sexual orientation

Sitting around the table after Thanksgiving dinner a couple years ago, my father says, "Heather, I have a question for you." "We [meaning my mother and he] figured you'd be the person to ask." I suppose I was "the person to ask" because I am an academic feminist, politically aware, and probably appear to know about a lot of nonmainstream stuff. "Are there really such things as bisexuals?" Wow–I wasn't prepared for this, especially on the fullest stomach of the year. I am reminded of the first week of classes freshman year of college, walking to class with my dear friend, Alex, who asks me out of the blue, "Heather, are there really such things as lesbians?" Mind you we were at Smith College in Northampton, Massachusetts. So it was pretty easy to laugh her off and assure her that, yes, Alex, there really are lesbians. But my Dad's question was a little harder to tackle.

First of all, bisexuality, unlike lesbianism, is not taken for granted by all but the most naïve of teens. People actually have debates about whether bisexuals–the Snuffaluffagus of sexualities–"really" exist. I had a feeling that one of such debates was about to erupt between my Dad and me. Second, I am bisexual myself, so while this does perhaps make me "the person to ask," I'm not sure a personal testimonial from his daughter was what my Dad had bargained for. But, I felt that I was faced with an opportunity–an opportunity to educate and spread the word–and if I did my job right, there would be one fewer naïve soul in the world. But I wasn't ready! On the spot like that, how could I articulate an argument convincing enough for my Dad?

The problem was what angle to take: how much ambiguity could my Dad really tolerate for this first educational lecture? Bisexuality alone is too ambiguous for many people to accept. That's why people keep trying to deny its existence, saying bisexuals are "really" gay but too afraid to accept it, or "really" straight but trying to be rebellious or "going through a phase." We prefer for everything to fit neatly into a category instead of straddling more than one.

As big-brained organisms, humans rely on a cognitive ordering of the vast amounts of information we encounter. As newborns, according to cognitive schema theory derived from the early work of Piaget (e.g., Piaget, 1936; Piaget & Inhelder, 1969), we begin to construct a framework to organize all the new information coming at us. Envision a cognitive map, like an ever-expanding flow chart with bubbles and arrows. Our tiny infant mind begins to draw arrows between the bubble for "Mom's scent" and the bubble for "Mom's sound" and the bubble for "Mom's look" and eventually we get a category, or a larger bubble for "Mom." We create cognitive categories, called schemas, for everything. We develop a category for "people," a category for "toys," a category for "dogs," each of which contains useful information about its members, such as "people pick you up," "toys make noise," "dogs lick your face." And this is extremely functional cognitively because it allows us to make inferences and predictions about novel members of a category without going through an extensive information-gathering process for each new thing we encounter. For example, the next time we meet a new furry, four-legged, floppy-eared creature on a leash that barks and wags its tail, we won't be at a loss to know what it is or to predict what it will do next. The few features we observe allow us to invoke our schema for dog and make inferences about what we haven't observed, such as, it eats dog biscuits, it does tricks, it's friendly, it licks your face. We don't have to observe all these things because our schema predicts them for us: thus, schemas are a cognitively efficient, time-saving device. We'd be lost without them.

Humans have been dependent on cognitive schemas for millennia, and we get uncomfortable when they get challenged. Things go much more smoothly for us when everything fits neatly into a category: a place for everything and everything in its place. What's the first thing everyone wants to know when a baby is born? Is it healthy? Does it have blue eyes? No! We need to know which *category* to put it in, according to an immensely important criterion in our society: gender. "The baby was born." *"What is it?"* We all know what is meant by that question. Hurry! A wet, naked newborn floating without a category!!! Quick! Should we place it in the "girl" schema or the "boy" schema?! Should we say it is "sweet" or that it is "strong"? Is it "robust" or is it "darling"? The schema will predict which characteristics to attribute, but we can only invoke the schema by knowing the gender. Lois Gould's 1972 "X: A Fabulous Child's Story" is an entertaining yet thought-provoking tale depicting our confusion and anger at not getting a straight answer to the question, "What is it?":

> Whenever the Joneses pushed Baby X's stroller in the park, smiling strangers would come over and coo: "Is that a boy or a girl?" The Joneses would smile back and say, "It's an X." The strangers would stop smiling then, and often snarl something nasty–as if the Joneses had snarled at *them*. (p. 83)

We need to categorize adults on the basis of gender as well. An ambiguous-gender person on the street: long hair, no make-up, baggy clothes or slim build, androgynous facial features . . . will undoubtedly be followed by whispers of "Is that a man or a woman?" We need to know. We need to know what category to place everyone in. The *Saturday Night Live* skits on "Pat" parody this desperate *need* to *know*. We need to categorize according to race too. The fair-skinned black or the "exotic" south Asian immigrant . . . hmmm . . . what *category* does she belong in? People feel it's a justifiable question: we need to know, don't we? We ask each other, "What is she?" We ask the ambiguous race person themselves, "What *are* you?" How many times must the biracial or multiracial person be asked to spell out her heritage for the purposes of others' categorization? We've heard Tiger Woods's racial make-up as many times as we've heard his golf scores. What if we asked ourselves, "What does it matter?" Why, exactly, do we need to know Tiger Woods's or Keanu Reeves's or Rae Dawn Chong's ancestry? Blank stares. We have no answer at all, do we? When I say we, I include myself: I'm as curious about Tiger Woods as the next person, although I have no earthly idea *why*. It's thousands of years of cognitive efficiency that compel us all to keep on categorizing.

A skit on *The Kids in the Hall* opens with women in their office cubicles gossiping. The new guy walks by. "Well, IS he or isn't he??!!" Giggles all around. This question is as clear as the "What is it?" question about a baby. We need to categorize people on the basis of sexual orientation as well as gender and race. We only have two schemas to choose from here: straight and gay, which is what makes bisexuality so problematic. Some people make it easy on us: a stereotypically feminine woman, married with children and a pretty manicure. Straight. A masculine, short-haired, make-up-free flannel-wearer with rainbow and pink triangle stickers on her truck. Lesbian. But woe to those who don't fit the textbook stereotypes!

What if she looks one way but "is" the other? What if he "says" he's straight but is a little too neat and likes to cook? Sex and gender and gender roles and sexual attraction and sexual behavior get jumbled and confused. Friends and acquaintances will stop at nothing to straighten it all out and discover the "truth."

I have a self-identified straight male friend who has lots of women friends but doesn't date much. He's attractive, smart, educated, funny, fun, and has a good job and yet, to his insisted chagrin, doesn't have a girlfriend. He's further "suspect" because he loves to talk on the phone for hours or just sit with a friend over cup after cup of coffee. He doesn't mind coming to the mall and helping me pick out shoes. He's sensitive. And most "telling" of all, he's homophobic (about men, anyway!). So my poor friend's ears burn as everyone wants to figure out his sexual orientation: "He seems like he could be gay, but I can't picture him with a man," "Maybe he's really gay but afraid to admit it to himself." It just can't be that he's who he is, perhaps straight, perhaps gay, perhaps bi, perhaps asexual (all of which suggesting that there is some "true" answer we could discover if we investigated hard enough)–OR defying stereotypes or categorization altogether, blazing some new path, or even suggesting a continuum or complex matrix of sexual orientation and gender and masculinity/femininity. Maybe instead of dichotomies of gay/straight; woman/man; masculine/feminine, there are infinite points and combinations–but suggesting this would make me a blasphemer against our beloved cognitive categorization.

I think its resistance to categorization is part of the reason bisexuality is so outcast. There are no real stereotypes to help identify bisexuals. No visual cues or markers that could tip off friends and family. No one's mother ever confronts them with "Honey, are you . . . bisexual?" There's no hairstyle, clothing, way of walking, way of talking, or tell-tale preference in music, entertainment, or choice of home lighting to help us categorize the next bisexual we meet. In other words, we don't really have a schema for bisexual and we find that very frustrating! We've tried to come up with a stereotype or two, such as bisexuals are nonmonogamous, but basically our bisexual schema is pretty bare. Not only is this cognitively inefficient, but it can be a little nerve-wracking, too: our best friend or the guy next to us on the bus or our roommate or our brother could be bi and we'd never know it! Yikes! It's easy to be homophobic, but it's harder to be bi-phobic when we don't know what we're looking for! Those bisexual people should have to wear a sign or something so we know to stay away from them! Without stereotypes of bisexuals, there can be no jokes ("How many bisexuals does it take to change a lightbulb?") or other "protections" that we use to berate outgroups and keep them in their place. I think so many people try to deny the existence of bisexuality because it's too ambiguous and schema-resistant and it defies all our best efforts to keep everyone neatly in a category.

I was afraid my Dad couldn't handle the ambiguity of a *third* type of sexual orientation. How is he supposed to get his brain around the ideas of bisexuality in addition to asexuality, multisexuality, omnisexuality, transsexuality . . . and the idea that labels and categories can't really capture what is going on with sexual orientation anyway? That it's a continuum or a multi-dimensional matrix or that it's *fluid*? This is a challenge that a schema-thinker does not want to face.

I've seen the way my students' brains start to hurt when their neat categories of sexual orientation are challenged. They can't quite grasp, for instance, the Native American *berdache* or two-spirit person: a person born with the biological sex of a male or a female, but not taking on the gender ordinarily associated with that sex, and participating in sexual activity with men and/or women while being considered neither straight nor gay. Berdache represents a different category: not woman, not man, not gay, not straight; simply berdache. That just doesn't map onto anything in mainstream American culture–but it does illuminate that sexual orientation and gender are socially constructed rather than given realities. We take it for granted that there are two genders or two sexual orientations, forgetting that we just made this up for our own cognitive convenience.

My students are also confused when I have them read a piece in which the author, a lesbian, discusses a hot sexual relationship she is having with a man; or a piece in which the bisexual author identifies as a lesbian; or pieces in which heterosexual feminists describe living celibate or lesbian lives for ideological reasons; or those in which sexual orientations and identities change and evolve over time. They expect everything to be consistent: desire, attraction, sexual activity, identifying labels–their schemas depend on such consistency–but reality can be a lot more complicated than this.

I mentioned earlier that I am bisexual, and I've slipped into this label and used it so much I almost forgot how I originally tried to reject it. Not because I didn't want to be attracted to members of both sexes–I thought that was great!–but because I felt that a label was missing the point. Growing up I assumed I was straight, as most of us do, and when I was about seventeen I discovered that some of the people I was attracted to were women. I was pretty excited about this. I thought it was neat to be open-minded, a free-thinker, to place other criteria for attraction above gender or sex. I frankly never considered referring to myself as "bisexual." It wasn't until later when the cumbersome "I'm open-minded, a free-thinker, I place other criteria for attraction above gender or sex!" left people confused that I began using the label "bisexual" for their cognitive convenience. But I still feel like it's missing something. I'm not hung up on gender or sex or sexual orientation, and I'm just attracted to whomever I'm attracted to. Does that make me a bisexual?

Really the label is kind of silly when you think about it. What's the definition anyway? "A bisexual is a person who is attracted to both men and women." *Any* men? *All* women? I asked a friend of mine why she uses the label "straight." "Because I'm attracted to men," she says. *"Any* men?" I ask. Are you attracted to your department chair? What about that guy Leon who lives down the street? Are you attracted to *my* husband?! Dick Cheney? Regis Philbin? A string of adamant "No!s" Well what men, then? How many? Maybe three or four? As a "bisexual," I don't currently have any women who I'm "attracted" to, and really only one man that I can think of right now. Sure, I have the *potential* to be attracted to more, either men or women, but frankly I'm a little wrapped up with my job, my social life, my summer plans, and trying to eat five fruits and vegetables every day. Who I'm attracted to and what gender they are doesn't particularly define me. I think it's funny that I have to have a label based on that.

I think forgetting that people are not attracted to every single person of one gender or another is what has lead to the myth of bisexual nonmonogamy. This idea that bisexuals cannot be monogamous because it would preclude sex with one gender is quite irrational when you think about it. For many bisexuals, bisexuality *means* that gender *doesn't* really matter that much. You're attracted to other things in a person before considering their genitalia or gender markers. Your lover is your lover first and a man or a woman second (or third or fourth, or somewhere way down the line on your list of things that matter about that person). Saying "bisexual people HAVE to have BOTH men and women–they can't be satisfied by just one" is saying that gender is THE thing that matters. More than anything else. It doesn't matter if you're kind and gentle and funny and intelligent and sensitive and interesting and attentive and affectionate and whatever else makes you a good lover–if you're only one gender, I *must* have other partners.[1] Absurd. This argument is implying that men and women are completely different from one another and there's no overlap. Any two men fall into the same category and any man and any woman must be put into different categories (there are those schemas again). Gender is the only relevant variable. If we admitted intra-gender variation, then we'd have to say we HAVE to have lovers from a variety of cultural and racial backgrounds–we can't be satisfied by only one . . . we HAVE to have both older and younger lovers–we can't be satisfied by only one . . . we have to have both Tom and Steve—we can't be satisfied by only one. Why should gender be more important than any other variable in a romantic or sexual partner? If you're straight, are all men the same? If you've had one, you've had them all? You can't be attracted to two very different men? If you can, then, according to the logic of the nonmonogamy myth, I guess you can't be monogamous. If I'm bi and I'm committed to a man, am I really more likely to be attracted to some specific woman and cheat with her than I am to be attracted to some specific other man and cheat with him? If I'm committed to a man, I forsake 100% of women—but I also forsake 99.999999% of men!! Who decided that for bisexual people gender is the one variable that matters in choosing partners? It's the one variable that *doesn't* matter.

So how do I explain all this to my Dad? He's a schema-dependent kind of guy. He's a man. He's straight. He's masculine. He's only ever been attracted to and intimate with women. He's been all these things all his life. Nice and neat. If you're gay, that's fine. That's a nice neat category too. But if you're bi, that's problematic. What is that? What category is that? How can you be *both* straight *and* gay? Is that a separate category, a combination of categories, or no category at all? Is there *really* such a thing as bisexuality, Heath, or are those people just confused? And if that's sticky, how do I sell him on these ideas of sexual fluidity, a 3-D sexual orientation matrix, or sexuality as a concept that defies labels? A lot of these things are too big for me to get my brain around too; I also have inherited the human inclination to label and categorize. But when I try to understand myself and the diversity of people around me, I can clearly see that just because we don't have a label for something, it doesn't mean it doesn't exist. In cognitive psychology, the Whorfian hypothesis suggests that language constrains thought: if we don't have a label or language to discuss something, then we really don't even consider the concept (Whorf, 1956). The abundant evidence supporting this hypothesis can be disheartening. But I find this hypothesis encouraging as well: if Whorf realized that our thinking is limited by our vocabulary, he thus also had the ability to see that there is a whole world of concepts that lie beyond our labels. This is encouraging in my thinking about my Dad, too, as is the cognitive schema theory that got me here in the first place. Schemas are meant to help us organize information; but they are also meant to be modified to accommodate new, sometimes contradictory information. I'm confident that this is true for my Dad's schemas. In fact, my plan is to give him a copy of this article and help him build a better schema for bisexuality—or better yet, to discard the schema altogether.

NOTE

1. This argument is not meant to espouse monogamy, only to insist that it is as possible for bisexual people as it is for straight or gay people. Many individuals (bi, straight, gay or otherwise) consciously choose polyamorous lifestyles, potentially having partners of different genders, personalities, and other attributes and choosing to have this variety for any number of personal, social, or political reasons. My point is that sexual orientation does not determine this choice.

REFERENCES

Gould, L. (1995). X: A fabulous child's story. In A. Kesselman, L. D. McNair, & N. Schniedewind (Eds.), *Women images and realities: A multicultural anthology* (pp. 82-87). Mountain View, CA: Mayfield.

Piaget, J. (1936). *The origins of intelligence in children.* NY: International University Press. (Reprinted in 1952).

Piaget, J., & Inhelder, B. (1969). *The psychology of the child.* NY: Basic.

Whorf, B. L. (1956). Science and linguistics. In J. B. Carroll (Ed.), *Language, thought, and reality: Selected writings of Benjamin Lee Whorf* (pp. 207-219). Cambridge, MA: MIT.

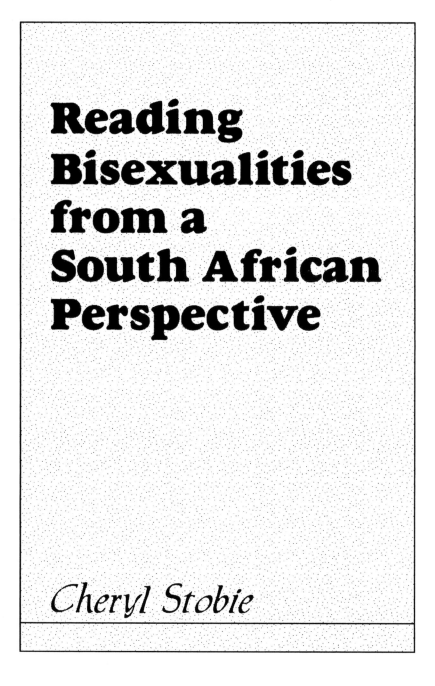

Reading Bisexualities from a South African Perspective

Cheryl Stobie

[Haworth co-indexing entry note]: "Reading Bisexualities from a South African Perspective." Stobie,
Cheryl. Co-published simultaneously in *Journal of Bisexuality* (Harrington Park Press, an imprint of The
Haworth Press, Inc.) Vol. 3, No. 1, 2003, pp. 33-52; and: *Women and Bisexuality: A Global Perspective* (ed:
Serena Anderlini-D'Onofrio) Harrington Park Press, an imprint of The Haworth Press, Inc., 2003, pp. 33-52.
Single or multiple copies of this article are available for a fee from The Haworth Document Delivery Service
[1-800-HAWORTH, 9:00 a.m. - 5:00 p.m. (EST). E-mail address: docdelivery@haworthpress.com].

SUMMARY. This article explores the absence of dialogue about bisexuality in South Africa and in the African continent. While South Africa's new Constitution explicitly vouchsafes protection on the grounds of "sexual orientation," leaders in a number of other African countries have called homosexuality un-African. I discuss the lack of a bisexual discourse in South Africa, and the prejudices and hostility directed towards bisexuals by lesbians and gays. I also examine a recent text, *Boy-wives and female husbands: Studies of African homosexualities*, edited by Stephen O. Murray and Will Roscoe, which debunks the myth that same-sex behavior is alien to Africa. There, bisexuality is treated dismissively despite the fact that those who have same-sex relations are frequently heterosexually married. I discuss the text as a feminist literary critic, commenting on the "techniques of neutralization" it employs. I argue that a sensitive definition of bisexuality would disrupt the impasse of binary categories while it would provide an appropriate framework to analyze sexualities in Africa and to better explore the experience of black women. *[Article copies available for a fee from The Haworth Document Delivery Service: 1-800-HAWORTH. E-mail address: <docdelivery@haworthpress.com> Website: <http://www.HaworthPress.com> © 2003 by The Haworth Press, Inc. All rights reserved.]*

KEYWORDS. Bisexuality, South Africa, Africa, *Boy-wives and female husbands*

I am a wind-swayed bridge, a crossroads inhabited by whirlwinds . . . You say my name is ambivalence? Think of me as Shiva, a many-armed and legged body with one foot on brown soil, one on white, one in straight society, one in the gay world, the man's world, the women's, one limb in the literary world, another in the working class, the socialist, and the occult worlds. A sort of spider woman hanging by one thin strand of web.

Who, me confused? Ambivalent? Not so. Only your labels split me.

–Gloria Anzaldúa, "La Prieta"

In this stirringly imaginative passage Gloria Anzaldúa evokes a hybrid yet unified creature, simultaneously animal, human and deity, whose creative body connects disparate domains, and who is only fragmented by others' labels. For me, this image of a figure that bridges brown and white soils, straight and gay society, and the worlds of men and women, yet refuses the label of ambivalence, is an inspiring metaphor of fluidity in sexual relations.

This fluidity, however, would be anathema to a number of African leaders who have expressed forceful opinions on variant sexualities. In 1995, Zimbabwean president, Robert Mugabe, banned the organization Gays and Lesbians of Zimbabwe (GALZ) from the country's International Book Fair. Terming homosexuality a repugnant Western import, he branded homosexuals as lower than pigs or dogs (*Mail & Guardian,* 1995, p. 15), and stated that "sodomites and perverts" had "no rights at all" (Welch, 2000, p. 12). In 1996, Namibian president, Sam Nujoma, urged the condemnation and rejection of homosexuals (Murray, 1998, p. 252). In October 2000, Namibia's Minister of Home Affairs, Jerry Ekandjo, urged 700 new police officers to "eliminate" gay men and lesbians "from the face of Namibia." He categorized homosexuality as unnatural and unAfrican (Amupadhi, 2000, p. 13). Nujoma has recently reiterated demands for the police to arrest, deport, and imprison gays and lesbians, even though the country has a liberal constitution ("Namibia 'does not allow gays,'" 2001, p. 4). Zambian president, Frederick Chiluba, has called for the arrest of lesbians and gays, as they fall foul of sodomy laws. Botswana too has sodomy laws, and a newly introduced law prohibiting lesbian sex. Last year, Ugandan president, Yoweri Museveni, ordered police to locate, charge and jail homosexuals. Kenyan president, Daniel arap Moi, declared that homosexuality was un-African and un-Christian (Luchsinger, 2000, p. 23).

The widespread scapegoating that has recently occurred in African countries is revealed in Museveni's warning: "Homosexuals are the ones provoking us. They are upsetting society. We shall not allow these people to challenge society" (*Natal Witness,* 1999). It has been suggested that homophobia is a useful weapon for leaders beleaguered by problems such as waning support, conflict, economic crises and the horrifying effects of the HIV/AIDS epidemic. Kamal Fizazi of the International Gay and Lesbian Human Rights Commission says, "Homophobia is a cultural campaign these leaders can initiate to detract attention from serious issues" (Luchsinger, 2000, pp. 23-24).

This "cultural campaign" has, however, triggered international protests and local activism. Despite harassment, blackmail, and arrests of members, GALZ membership is burgeoning. GALZ activist Tsitsi Tiripano, internationally known for her speaking tours, received recognition by being named one of Amnesty International's 50 Human Rights Defenders in 1998. Tiripano initially chose to use a pseudonym for reasons of security, but she continues to use it because she is known by it internationally and because of its meaning. She explains, *"Tsitsi* means 'mercy,' *tiripano* means 'we're here.' Everyone must have mercy with gays and lesbians because we're here." She has revealed her real name, Poliyana Mangwiro. In response to the claim that homosexuality is un-African, Tiripano points to the existence of the Shona word, *ngochani,* which she translates as "homosexual" (Welch, 2000, pp. 12-14), thus pointing to the existence of same-sex relationships in Zimbabwe before colonialism.

As well as being homophobic, societies in Africa are patriarchal, so lesbians and bisexual women particularly challenge the *status quo,* and face social reprisals. For instance, when another GALZ activist, Tina Machida, came out to her parents as a lesbian at the age of 18, they arranged for her to be raped in the hopes of "normalizing" her (Luchsinger, 2000, p. 24). However, the strength of survivors and activists acts as an inspiration to others. Tiripano escaped from an unwanted arranged marriage with a man 40 years her senior, taking her two children with her. She proudly claims a lesbian identity (Welch, 2000, p. 15). Other Zimbabwean women, inspired by her courageous example, came out to her, "but most of them are married. They say that they can't leave their children because of financial reasons. So they stay with their husbands because of that but some are bisexual now" (Rodgerson, 2000, p. 29).

Other African countries that have successfully organized against homophobic politicians include Namibia, Zambia and Botswana. In Namibia, women such as Elizabeth Khaxas of the feminist collective Sister Namibia have been particularly effective. In 1997, the collective launched the Rainbow Project, a pressure group for gay, lesbian, bisexual, transsexual and transgender rights (Luchsinger, 2000, p. 24). In 1998 a report appeared of the inception of a Zambian group, Lesbians, Gays, Bisexual and Transgender Persons Association (Legatra), to counter harassment and victimization (Kunda, 1998). It is noteworthy that one of the constituent elements ("bi") disappears in the chosen acronym, although it is gratifying to see the inclusiveness of the Rainbow Project and Legatra. In Botswana, newspaper stories based on the lives of men and women have challenged the myth that homosexuality is un-African (Murray, 1998, pp. 253-254).

In a number of African countries, then, homophobia, threats, victimization and oppression have had the opposite of their intended effect. During the era of the apartheid Nationalist government in South Africa (1948-1994), a similar pattern was enacted. In a society that was not only homophobic, but also racist and sexist, the most vocal and well-organized group during this period consisted of white, middle-class, urban gay men. The relative privilege of this group of homosexuals did not, however, protect them from the normalizing power of "Christian National" hegemony. For example, the *Mail and Guardian* newspaper has recently brought before a wide audience research on human rights abuses in the South African Defence Force. In an effort to stamp out "deviance," mostly white male conscripts, but also women, were subjected to electric shocks in the process of aversion therapy, as well as chemical castration, and gender reassignment surgery, some of which was not completed (Kirk, 2000, pp. 4-5).

As revealed in *The invisible ghetto: Lesbian and gay writing from South Africa* (Krouse & Berman, 1993) and *Defiant desire: Gay and lesbian lives in South Africa* (Gevisser & Cameron, 1994); however, despite institutionalized pressure and prejudice, men and women across the spectrum of what Archbishop Desmond Tutu has memorably called our "Rainbow Nation" have established social spaces to be queer.

These texts give evidence of the lives of same-sex lovers of varied ethnic backgrounds, ranging from, amongst others, cross-racial working class couples, "coloured" (mixed-race) schoolchildren and drag queens, white intellectuals, black youths from the townships, sex-workers, mine-workers, and lesbian *sangomas* (traditional healers). Their stories confound claims that homosexuality is "un-African." Despite this variety, however, women are significantly less represented than men. Bisexuality is poorly represented, with some notable exceptions. One of these exceptions is a number of references to the system of same-sex "mine-marriages" between older and younger miners, and glancing allusions to the wives or girlfriends of these men. A second exception is a poignant story about a threesome consisting of two women and a man, "Bye bye, forget me not," by Welma Odendaal, from *The invisible ghetto*. A third account of bisexuality occurs in *Defiant desire*, a brief autobiographical sketch by Zubeida, in which she discusses her bisexual identity, the oppression she experiences, and her perception of prejudice in lesbian and gay organizations. It is noteworthy that in a rare instance when the word "bisexual" actually occurs, in the name of the organization ABIGALE (Association of Bisexuals, Gays and Lesbians), no evidence occurs in the text of actual bisexual individuals in the group: only gays and lesbians are referred to. Conversely, when bisexual behaviour is described, it is generally not referred to as such.

Over the apartheid era, a shift occurred from social/supportive groups to gay activism, the tempo increasing as the apartheid machine was dismantled. At the same time, such influences as a growing democratic movement and feminism led to expressions of dissatisfaction and feelings of exclusion from blacks and women within the queer community, and a number of organizations underwent radical transformation. Queers also worked for rights within political groups.

After South Africa's transition to democracy in 1994, much gay and lesbian activism, spearheaded by the National Coalition for Gay and Lesbian Equality (NCGLE), centred around staving off pressure from religious fundamentalists and ensuring that the Constitution of 1996, uniquely in the world, enshrine rights on the basis of "sexual orientation." This success provides grounds for confidence but not complacency.

Significant gains have been won. The climate of opinion is more open, and there is less overt homophobia. Political triumphs for the NCGLE include a successful challenge of the sodomy laws, the Constitutional Court declaring same-sex laws unconstitutional, and achieving policies of nondiscrimination in the Defence Force and equal rights for homosexuals at work. Discrimination is illegal on a range of grounds, including sexual orientation. Issues of legally-recognized same-sex partnerships and the possibility of marriage are being debated (ILGA, 1999). The Constitutional Court has overturned the ban on same-sex partners of South Africans settling in this country (*Diva,* 2000, p. 23). A number of gays have sought asylum in South Africa because in their home countries (including Ghana and Uganda), their safety is jeopardized. A new South African law makes sexual orientation sufficient grounds for political asylum (ILGA, 1999).

Freedom of expression has improved since the overturning of the Obscene Photographic Matter Act, which banned the possession of visual depictions of various sexual acts (ILGA, 1999). The stringent censorship of the past has been lifted, and television programmes such as the film of Vito Russo's *The celluloid closet* and local productions such as Greta Schiller's *The man who drove with Mandela*, Jack Lewis's *From Sando to Samantha* and Zackie Achmat's *Apostles of civilized vice* have been aired.

Most of the queer television programmes seen in this country focus more specifically on men than women. There is general evidence, however, of a growing visibility of lesbians. One example is the newspaper profile of Zodwa Shongwe of a theatre in Johannesburg, who has achieved a balance between being out of the closet as a lesbian and having a traditional African belief system (Coleman, 1999). Another black woman who proudly claims her lesbian identity as a South African is Phumi Mtetwa, ILGA co-secretary. She has said, "The rights of women not to be discriminated against on the basis of sexuality are, and should be seen to be, indivisible from the goals of the broader women's human rights movement. The struggle for equality, peace and democracy cannot move forward whilst particular groups are stigmatised, marginalised and rendered invisible with little or no recourse" ("Threat to women's freedom," 2000). Recently, Mtetwa has also rebuked opponents of gay rights at the Beijing +5 United Nations conference, including an angry Nigerian (woman) Member of Parliament and a bemused Ugandan (woman) Minister of State for Gender. Mtetwa maintained, "To penalise people for being what they are is profoundly disrespectful," and scotched the old refrain that lesbianism is un-African by proudly affirming, "I am an African" (Haffajee, 2000).

Queer women have been targeted by a new, slim magazine, *Women on Women*, which joins *Exit*, *Outright* and *Gay SA*, which cater mainly if not exclusively to men. Billed as "leading in style, progressive in content," this is a worthwhile venture, although it remains to be seen if it will be commercially viable. Interestingly, the editor, Sharon Cooper, has made an appeal for the healing of divisions caused by discrimination and prejudice within the community of queer women, such as racism, and antagonism by "real" lesbians towards bisexuals (2000, p. 2).

For those of us fortunate enough to have Internet access (and this is a small sector in South Africa), the exchange of ideas is stimulating and provides support. E-mail lists, in particular, provide virtual communities, which transcend geographical boundaries. Specifically, South African queer Websites are thin on the ground, but include *Behind the mask,* a Website on gay and lesbian affairs in (Southern) Africa at <http://www.mask.org.za>, the *Mail and Guardian* newspaper's <http://www.q.co.za>, and the *Gay and Lesbian Archives* <http://www.wits.ac.za/gala/>.

In the culture of democracy since 1994 in South Africa, human rights have been expanded and queers have more legal protection and freedom of expression than ever before. However, prejudice obviously still exists, as do legal anomalies. For instance, there is still a discrepancy between the age of consent for heterosexual acts (16 years) and same-sex sexual contact (19 years). HIV/AIDS is an escalating, desperate problem for everyone in this country, regardless of sexual orientation. Much misinformation and fear surround this epidemic. In December 1998, a woman, Gugu Dlamini, was murdered near Durban because of her open disclosure of her HIV-positive status (Nicodemus, 1999). Rejection and stigmatization frequently occur.

In August 1999, a gay man, Le Roux Theunnisen, and his estranged father were interviewed on a television programme. Two days after the programme was aired, Theunnisen was murdered (ILGA, 1999). In November 1999, Cape Town's Blah Bar was targeted for a pipe-bomb attack, during which nine people were injured. The owner attributed the attack to homophobia *(Diva,* 2000, p. 23). In the year 2000 in South Africa, then, there is the potential for new insights into sexuality, although violence, prejudice and homophobia still oppress those who are part of sexual minorities.

* * *

Turning more specifically to bisexuality, one of the problem areas in South Africa is the ubiquity of the homosexual-heterosexual binary. Often precise terms are eschewed in favour of the binarist either-or, which leads to a lack of visibility of individuals such as bisexuals. In the "Directory of bisexual and bi-inclusive groups" section of the 2000 edition of the *Bisexual resource guide,* edited by Robyn Ochs, four local groups are listed: the Gay and Lesbian Organization of the Witwatersrand, based in Johannesburg, which does not include "bisexual" in its name; Cape Town's Association of Bisexuals, Gays and Lesbians (ABIGALE), which focuses mainly on gays and lesbians; Durban's Lesbian, Gay and Bisexual Collective; and Johannesburg's Fata Morgana, billed as a "support group for married gay men" (1999, p. 157).

This reluctance to name as bisexuals men who act in a bisexual manner is fairly common. A typical reference is one by Mark Gevisser, who refers to " 'Phil,' a gay man who lived with his wife and children in Soweto" (2000, p. 16). In the circumstances, the adjective "bisexual" might be more appropriate. Unproblematically claiming "Phil" as gay would seem to be an act of appropriation.

As an informal gauge of the availability of information on different sections of queer subculture, I looked up keywords in the catalogue of the library of the local university, the University of Natal (Pietermaritzburg campus), where I work. This is the number of books with titles containing the following words:

gay/s	149
lesbian/s	83
lesbian/s and gay/s	56
homosexual/ity	42
queer	19
bisexual/s or bisexuality	14
bisexuals, lesbian/s and gay/s	5
transgender	2
transgender, bisexual, lesbian and gay	1

From this list, it can be inferred that considerably more information is available about men than women, and more books in the library focus on a specific group rather than focussing on a range of groups. Transgenders are particularly poorly represented, but fewer than 10% of texts focus on bisexuals as compared with gays. I also consulted the archive of the *Mail and Guardian* Website. The *Mail and Guardian* is a weekly South African newspaper with a reputation for being progressive and searching. The keywords and number of hits from 1 January 1998 to mid-2000 are as follows:

gay	245
lesbian	91
bisexual	14

The word "gay" may occasionally be used in a gender-neutral way, but most often it refers to men. The online pattern of relative bisexual invisibility is similar to the pattern in the library cited.

* * *

Having set the scene with this brief geographical discussion, let me shift briefly to the realm of discourse. In Western discourse, at least since the time of Plato, one of the main structuring paradigms has been that of binary oppositions. This long philosophical history of binarisms is particularly associated with Cartesian dualism and the rationality esteemed by the Enlightenment. This patterning persists in many areas up to the present, despite competing ideologies provided by postmodernism. Language, in general, has been made a repository of binaries. Literary criticism is replete with heroes and anti-heroes; novels and anti-novels; plays and anti-plays; antinomies such as the Apollonian and the Dionysian; and structural devices such as doppelgangers.

Recently the celebrated novelist, Margaret Atwood, has been quoted on the subject of literature and binaries:

> Duality particularly interests fiction as a form. It is particularly interesting from the word go-by which I mean Cain and Abel, Romulus and Remus. It's the structure of siblings. Look at Christianity–having had God, they had to have the Devil. I think it's the structure of the body and the brain. Two hands, two eyes, two halves of the brain–but one heart. This has been something that has interested people writing about being human. (Viner, 2000, p. 35)

Whatever the genesis of this deep-seated impulse towards binarist discourse, however, there is also a recent intellectual current that questions its legitimacy. Derrida has amply demonstrated that an epistemology based upon binaries is hierarchical, with one term being privileged at the expense of the other. Attempting to disrupt the system by elevating the oppressed term simply inverts the orthodoxy, and continues the impasse. Deconstruction attempts to dismantle the system by disrupting the binaries that underpin it. Derrida muses about the consequences of disrupting "the code of sexual marks," beyond oppositions. He expresses his desire to "believe in the multiplicity of sexually marked voices" beyond "an implacable destiny which immures everything for life in the figure 2" (Derrida & McDonald, 1982, p. 76).

French theorists of femininity, following Derrida's deconstruction and Lacan's psychoanalysis, have attempted to subvert hierarchized oppositions of, for instance, day/night, law/nature, man/woman, public/private, white/black, and nondisabled/disabled. They have attempted to show that these are not natural and immutable distinctions, but are provisional and disruptible discursive mechanisms. One way in which such theorists as Cixous and Kristeva have queried hierarchies is by using tropes of pluralism, hybridity and bisexuality.

Shildrick and Price maintain: "In contesting the universal signification of the living body our aim should be to acknowledge the plurality of possible constructions and the multiple differences which exceed imposed normativities" (Shildrick & Price, 1999, p. 439).

So far I have been discussing binaries in Western culture, but it is important to note that this is a culture-specific paradigm. Gender is not necessarily viewed in binary terms in other cultures. For example, North-American Native cultures frequently conceptualised three or four genders. Documentation suggests that 155 of these cultures had a third gender (which consisted of biological males assuming female roles), and a smaller number a fourth (consisting of biological females assuming male roles) (Dean, 2000). These third or fourth genders are sometimes called two-spirit people, or by the outsider term of "Berdaches."

Within the field of anthropology, in the heady but, from this time-perspective, somewhat grand-narrativizing days of early second-wave feminism, articles appeared such as Sherry Ortner's "Is female to male as nature is to culture?" (1974). Critiques swiftly exposed the rigidity of the binary framework of culture/nature and private/public as being ethnocentric, falsely universalizing and essentializing in claiming that all societies of all times followed such patterns.

However, what the spate of feminist-based research pointed to was a number of significant omissions, distortions and trivializations in the field of anthropology/ethnography with regard to gender. Questions asked and assumptions made often reflected a deep androcentric bias in the researchers.

For a generation, attempts have been made in the general academic milieu, and specifically in anthropology, to unsettle binaries, in terms of gender, sexuality, roles and race. In the last decade these attempts have intensified through the work of Queer theorists, among others.

* * *

This, then, is the background for my examination of the book with the tantalizing title: *Boy-wives and female husbands: Studies of African homosexualities*, edited by Stephen O. Murray and Will Roscoe (1998). What I hoped for from the book was a further refutation of the common charge of homosexuality being "un-African," which I have discussed. I also hoped for breadth and inclusiveness in an interpretation of queerness, as promised by the plural "homosexualities." I should mention that I am reading this primarily anthropological text as a feminist and a lecturer in English and Gender Studies, not as an anthropologist. From this perspective, I found that *Boy-wives and female husbands* met my first criterion: it offers a range of texts from the 18th to the late 20th centuries, which examine a considerable number of sub-Saharan cultures, and provides ample evidence of variant sexual practices being indigenous over a long period. There is much fascinating material, including translations of ethnographic accounts of pre-colonial and colonial times, court records of male homosexual "crime" in early colonial Zimbabwe, same-sex marriages, the concept of "male lesbians" in Hausa (the most common language in West Africa), adolescent same-sex sexual behaviour, cross-dressing, role reversal, and women who love women in Lesotho. Also of interest is an appendix with a list of 50-odd African cultures with same-sex patterns, most of which have local terms for same-sex sexual practices or roles.

Frustratingly, the book offers no biographical information on authors, but it would seem that only one of the 12 authors is a black African. Another African, a Kikuyu man living in San Francisco, is interviewed in another chapter. There are two women contributors, one of whom focuses on men, the other on women. There is also a discussion of woman-woman marriage in Africa. Africans are represented by and large as the subjects, not the agents, of study, and women are un-derrepresented, as the editors acknowledge.

As far as my second criterion is concerned, then, while a range of lo-cal manifestations of male homosexuality is explored in the text, the gamut of homosexualities is not fully explored. Reviewer Gert Hekma charges the editors with negligence in not ensuring a better gender bal-ance, and deplores the omission of any reference to a 1985 book by E. Tietmeyer on the subject of marriage between women, *Studien zur gynaegamie in Afrika* (1999).

A further omission is glaringly apparent in the light of the constant emphasis throughout the text that, in Africa, heterosexual marriage and procreation are strongly enforced social obligations. A husband's clan-destine affairs with women or men may be tolerated in various cultures, and there is evidence for same-sex erotic relationships between co-wives, and between married women in Lesotho. It is striking, how-ever, that despite the use of terms such as "gay" and "lesbian" by con-temporary authors, there is an avoidance of the term "bisexual."

Techniques of neutralization. The effect of this avoidance seems to be consonant with Amber Ault's discussion of "techniques of neutral-ization" (1996, pp. 207-208) used by a relatively powerful discourse to neutralize another. In this case, the discourse of "homosexuality" or "gay and lesbian" enquiry suppresses a more nuanced account, which includes other variant sexualities. Ault discusses four strategies em-ployed in this process: suppression, incorporation, marginalization, and delegitimization. These strategies rely on a system of binaries to achieve their effects. I intend to apply these four categories to certain aspects of *Boy-wives and female husbands.*

Suppression. In mainstream society, the assumption is made that sub-jects are heterosexual, and queer subjects, if they exist at all, are per-ceived as Other, or marginal to this hegemony. In terms of sexuality, heteronormativity is the dominant discourse. Adrienne Rich has re-ferred to this as "compulsory heterosexuality" (1980, pp. 631-660). In a manoeuvre designed to escape the tyranny of this heteronormativity, gay and lesbian writers deliberately attempt to overturn the centre/mar-gin binary. In so doing, however, they have a tendency to centralize their own experience as lesbians and gays, inadvertently suppressing other categories of queers in the process. They do this by substituting the tyranny of compensatory "compulsory" monosexuality (James, 1996, p. 222), by privileging same-sex relations above opposite-sex re-lations sanctioned by heteronormativity. This results in the suppression of the category of bisexuality. According to Paula Rust, "bisexuality is only invisible because it is not seen . . . The failure to see bisexuality lies in the observer, not the observed" (1992, p. 299). This suppression is distressing for, and disrespectful towards, those whose behaviour transgresses these either/or paradigms.

There are a number of examples of this myopia in *Boy-wives and female husbands*, resulting in distortion. Rudolf P. Gaudio, in "Queer lesbians and other queer notions in Hausa," uses the label "gay" to describe men who marry and have children, and who have sex with men. He acknowledges that their construction of their behaviour differs from that of Western gay men, but applies the term because of his subjects' self-conscious behaviour. He comments, "Hausa people generally refer to homosexuality as an act rather than a psychological drive or predisposition, and homosexual men are more often described as men who *do* homosexuality than as men who *want* other men sexually" (1998, pp. 117-8). Behaviour, then, is the yardstick employed in Hausa society. However, Gaudio declines to use the concept of bisexuality:

> I have chosen not to use the term *bisexual* to refer to married gay Hausa men because I understand bisexuality to refer to an individual's acknowledged capacity to be sexually attracted to both women and men and to the assertion of one's prerogative to act on such attraction; this implies a degree of choice regarding sexual matters that is not recognized in Hausa society. Specifically, most Hausa people do not see marriage as a choice but rather as a moral and social obligation. (1998, p. 118)

However, if these people's emphasis on behaviour, rather than choice, were heeded, and if bisexuals' own definitions of bisexuality (such as James's "bisexuality is . . . the sexual or intensely emotional, although not necessarily concurrent or equal, attraction of an individual to members of more than one gender" (1996, p. 218) were applied, bisexuality would seem to come closer to describing the behaviour of these Hausa men, and that of many other people described in *Boy-wives and female husbands*.

It is not only Gaudio, however, who suppresses the concept of bisexuality. The editors, Stephen O. Murray and Will Roscoe, ignore the concept in their four overview sections of the book and their conclusion, except in parenthetical reference. The term does not even occur in the index (a classic means of rendering a concept invisible). However, anthropological literature provides a number of examples of bisexual behaviour in various cultures world-wide (although the term "bisexuality" is not used as an organizational framework). This evidence ruptures easy binaries. Half a century ago, C.S. Ford and F.A. Beach commented:

> When it is realised that 100 percent of the males in certain societies engage in homosexual as well as heterosexual alliances, and when it is understood that many men and women in our own society are equally capable of relations with partners of the same or opposite sex . . . then it should be clear that one cannot classify homosexual and heterosexual tendencies as being mutually exclusive or even opposed to each other. (1951, in Fox, p. 11)

Margaret Mead emphasized the ubiquity of bisexuality, noting that "even a superficial look at other societies and some groups in our own society should be enough to convince us that a very large number of human beings–probably a majority–are bisexual in their potential capacity for love" (1975, pp. 6-7).

Given the general reluctance of anthropologists to employ bisexuality as a conceptual category, even when the evidence would make its use logical, and even when writers point to the need to examine the totality of sexual expression within a given culture (Fox, 1996, p. 13), it is perhaps not entirely surprising that Murray and Roscoe remain loyal to the homosexual-heterosexual binary. However, where logic is abandoned, and professional requirements of evidence and accurate labelling are ignored, quite obviously a high degree of denial is revealed, and the end result is to further entrench theoretical binaries that do not adequately address subjects' lived experience. It is interesting that in 1993 Jo Eadie criticized Murray's essay on Mesoamerica for suppressing the possibility of bisexuality by insisting on using the dichotomous paradigm (Plummer, 1992). However, either Murray was unaware of this criticism, or he chose to ignore it.

In 1996, "Bisexuality in the Arab world: An interview with Muhammed" by François Gollain appeared (Rose, Stevens et al., 1996, pp. 58-61). Muhammed notes that a bisexual *identity* is not found in the Arab world, although bisexuality is a widespread practice. He claims that almost all Arab men are bisexual, but very few women. He maintains that women do not know about men's bisexuality as they are unaware of men's private domain. The question arises as to what extent the men may be ignorant of the women's private domain. It is possible that there could be a same-sex erotic realm for women, consonant with Elaine Showalter's "wild zone" (1986, pp. 243-270). Showalter adapts a model of two overlapping circles developed by anthropologist Edwin Ardener, consisting of dominant/male and muted/female. According to this model, male consciousness is dominant, structured by language and knowable, even in the crescent where the dominant/male and muted/female circles do not intersect. However, in the female-only crescent, the repressed and the revolutionary may find expression, unbeknownst to the dominant/male group.

Incorporation. In her chapter, "'When a woman loves a woman' in Lesotho: Love, sex and female husbands" (Murray & Roscoe, 1998, pp. 223-241), Kendall unearths something akin to the "wild zone." She observes women exchanging erotic kisses, and she learns of a range of sexual practices between women. These are not, however, referred to as having sex, as the ur-signifier in a sexual act defined as such is the penis. She discovers that (heterosexual) marriage is universal, but that around 1950 socially endorsed relationships between pairs of married women were common, although this practice is now waning.

It is a pleasure for a woman reader to encounter a chapter in this book that focuses on women, and the material is fascinating. I had an additional interest in this chapter, as Kendall lectured at the university where I lecture and I knew her slightly. I admired her for her openness, for her adoption of two Basotho daughters, for her energy, her creative writing and her scholarship. I have no desire to enter into an adversarial relationship with Kendall, to upset her friends or to expose myself to criticism for being unsisterly. Fortunately, Kendall, herself, has come to my rescue. A report by Maganthrie Pillay on Kendall's reading of this chapter as a paper at the Southern African Gay and Lesbian Studies Colloquium relates how she invited a critical response from the audience (1996, pp. 99-100). With respect, then, I offer my critical response.

Incorporation refers to the practice of gays and lesbians of appropriating bisexuals as members of their own groups. For instance, Sue George (1993, p. 38) and Emma Donoghue (herself a lesbian) refer to the incorporation techniques of ground-breaking author Lillian Faderman, who ignores evidence of different-sex relationships as she "pressgang[s] clearly bisexual women into the all-star exclusively-lesbian history pageant" (1996, pp. 75-76).

In "'When a woman loves a woman' in Lesotho," Kendall does not once consider the framework of bisexuality to examine the experiences of (heterosexually) married women who have erotic relationships with other women; instead, she refers to "lesbian or lesbian-like behaviour" (p. 237). Given the fact that to call these women lesbian does them the injustice of privileging part of their experience at the expense of another, and given the fact that Kendall's attempts to explain her own lesbianism to women in Lesotho were met with incredulity, this incorporation seems to me to weaken an otherwise fine paper.

Marginalization. This technique of neutralization occurs when bisexuality is mentioned, but on the sidelines of the main discourse. In an article translated from the German, Kurt Falk's "Homosexuality among the natives of Southwest Africa" dating from the 1920s, this claim is dropped: "My opinion is that the percentage among the natives able to consort with both sexes and (according to the evidence of many natives questioned about it) feel the same desire for both is around 90 percent" (p. 196). The editors of *Boy-wives and female husbands*, Murray and Roscoe, make no reference to this opinion, although they discuss Falk in some detail. Without contextualization, Falk's claim recedes into the margins.

Delegitimization. This process occurs when gays and lesbians discredit bisexual experience. The whiff of biphobia is strong in the interview of Kamau, a young Kikuyu, by Stephen Murray. Murray appears edgy whenever Kamau talks of women, and refuses to validate his range of experiences. For instance, Kamau's comment about his relationship with his girlfriend, "We both enjoy it, the sex," provokes the amazing conversational leap of, "So, there are no gay bars in Nairobi" (p. 62). The absence of a question mark highlights what appears to be an attempt to wrench the conversation from a distasteful track.

There are a number of attempts to show that while marriage is a social obligation, the partners (and the focus is more specifically on the male partners) may have no desire for their spouses or the other sex in general. However, Kamau attests to his emotional and sexual responses to both sexes: "I love being with men and I love girls" (p. 53). This message, however, does not appear to be one that the book wishes to endorse.

Boy-wives and female husbands is a useful, but flawed, first book on the subject of African homosexualities. It may give comfort to Africans and diasporan Africans who have been plagued with guilt about being contaminated by "foreign perversity." However, further texts about sexualities in Africa need to pay more attention to the experiences of women and to the use of bisexuality as a conceptual framework, which might unsettle stultifying binaries in a context where they are especially inappropriate.

I am not proposing the use of the term "bisexual/ity" in a universalizing or essentializing way. It needs to be applied with respect and care, bearing in mind the differences between identity, behaviour, and potential. However, it must be remembered that some people of African descent, both within and outside the continent, themselves claim the term, and that some writers about African sexuality have displayed biphobia by ignoring the evidence and imposing terms such as "gay" and "lesbian" on behaviour that does not warrant it. Bisexualities in Africa generally may differ from the concept elsewhere in the world, but they need to be accorded respectful treatment along with other African homosexualities.

Finally, I urge more awareness of the range of sexualities in South Africa, and a challenging of practices that reinscribe inaccurate binaries. A sharpening of categories used by popular anthropologists is necessary. Wariness on the part of readers is necessary. There also needs to be more focus on the experiences of women, particularly written by women themselves. Sensitivity and empathy are required for us to inhabit imaginatively the body of Gloria Anzaldúa's hybrid spider-woman, negotiating multiple vectors of identity, and refusing the tyranny of binaries.

NOTE

1. A term used in another context by sociologists Gresham Sykes and David Matza (1957) in "Techniques of neutralization," *American Sociological Review, 22,* 664-670 (Ault, 1996, p. 207).

REFERENCES

Amupadhi, T. (2000, October 6-12). Eliminate homosexuals, says minister. *Mail & Guardian*, p. 13.

Anzaldúa, G. (1983). La prieta. In C. Moraga & G. Anzaldúa (Eds.), *This bridge called my back: Writings by radical women of color.* New York: Kitchen Table Press.

Ault, A. (1996). Hegemonic discourse in an oppositional community: Lesbian feminist stigmatization of bisexual women. In B. Beemyn & M. Eliason. (Eds.), *Queer studies: A lesbian, gay, bisexual and transgender anthology.* New York: New York University Press.

Coleman, R. (1999, November 3). Coming to terms with being lesbian and being African is a mean feat. *Mail & Guardian*, q online. *www.q.co.za/regulars/coleman/991015-shongwe.htm>.*

Cooper, S. (2000, May). Editorial note. *Women on Women, 3,* 2.

Dean, D. M. (2000, October). Dualism's just a construct. H-Net book review. *<H-Minerva@h-net.msu.edu>.*

Derrida, J., & McDonald, C. V. (1982, summer). Choreographies. *Diacritics: A review of contemporary criticism*, 76.

Diva. (2000, February). 23.

Donoghue, E. (1996). Divided heart, divided history: Eighteenth century bisexual heroines. In S. Rose, C. Stevens et al. (Eds.), *Bisexual horizons: Politics, histories, lives*. London: Lawrence & Wishart.

Ford, C. S., & Beach, F. A. (1951). *Patterns of sexual behavior*. New York: Harper & Row. Quoted in R.C. Fox (1996). Bisexuality in perspective: A review of theory and research. In B.A. Firestein (Ed.). *Bisexuality: The psychology and politics of an invisible minority*. Thousand Oaks: Sage Publications.

Fox, R.C. (1996). Bisexuality in perspective: A review of theory and research. In B.A. Firestein (Ed.), *Bisexuality: The psychology and politics of an invisible minority*. Thousand Oaks: Sage Publications.

George, S. (1993). *Women and bisexuality*. London: Scarlet Press.

Gevisser, M. (2000, January 2). Love will tear us apart. *Sunday Times* Millennium Souvenir, p.16.

Gevisser, M., & Cameron, E. (Eds.), (1994). *Defiant desire: Gay and lesbian lives in South Africa*. Johannesburg: Ravan Press.

GLA to change its name. (2000, July 12). *The Natal Witness*, p. 2.

Gollain, F. (1996). Bisexuality in the Arab world: An interview with Muhammed. In S. Rose, C. Stevens et al. (Eds.), *Bisexual horizons: Politics, histories, lives*. London: Lawrence & Wishart.

Haffajee, F. (2000, June 8). Uneasy bedfellows fight sexual rights. *Flamme: African daily newspaper*. *<www.womensnet.org.za/beijing5/news1/news1.cfm>* Gennet listerv 12 June 2000.

Hekma, G. (1999). African homosexualities: A review. *Thamyris*. *<http://altern.org/semgai/articles/Murray_par_Hekma.html>*.

ILGA (The international lesbian and gay association) Website: World legal survey. (1999). *<www.ilga.org/Information/legal_survey/africa/southafrica.htm>*.

James, C. (1996). Denying complexity: The dismissal and appropriation of bisexuality in queer, lesbian, and gay theory. In B. Beemyn & M. Eliason (Eds.), *Queer studies: A lesbian, gay, bisexual and transgender anthology*. New York: New York University Press.

Kendall. (1986). From lesbian heroine to devoted wife: Or, what the stage would allow. In M. Kehoe (Ed.), *Historical, literary and erotic aspects of lesbianism* (pp. 9-21). London: Harrington Park Press.

Kirk, P. (2000, July 28-August 3). Mutilation by the military. *Mail & Guardian*, pp. 4-5.

Krouse, M., & Berman, K. (Eds.). (1993). *The invisible ghetto: Lesbian and gay writing from South Africa*. Johannesburg: COSAW Publishing.

Kunda, A. (1998, September 11). Zambian gays out of closet. *Mail & Guardian*.

Luchsinger, G. (2000, April/May). Out in Africa. *Ms, 10.3*, 23-24.

Mail & Guardian. (1995, August 4-10). p. 15.

Mead, M. (1975, January). Bisexuality: What's it all about? *Redbook*, 6-7.

Murray, S. O. (1998). Sexual politics in contemporary Southern Africa. In S.O. Murray & W. Roscoe (Eds.), *Boy-wives and female husbands: Studies of African homosexualities*. Houndmills: Macmillan Press.

Murray, S.O., & Roscoe, W. (Eds.). (1998). *Boy-wives and female husbands: Studies of African homosexualities*. Houndmills: Macmillan Press.

Namibia "does not allow gays." (2001, March 21). *The Natal Witness*, p. 4.

The Natal Witness. (1999, November 20).

Nicodemus, A. (1999, May 7). Africa still stigmatises HIV-positive. *Weekly Mail*. <www.sn.apc.org/wmail/issues/990507/NEWS34.html>.

Ochs, R. (Ed.). (1999). *Bisexual resource guide*. Cambridge, MA: Bisexual Resource Center.

Ortner, S. B. (1974). Is female to male as nature is to culture? In M. Z. Rosaldo & L. Lamphere (Eds.), *Woman, culture and society* (pp. 67-87). Stanford, CA: Stanford University Press.

Pillay, M. (1996). Gay and lesbian academics are everywhere. *Agenda, 28*, 99-100.

Plummer, K. (Ed.). (1992). *Homosexualities*. London: Routledge. Cited in J. Eadie (1993). Activating bisexuality: Towards a bi/sexual politics. In J. Bristow & A.R. Wilson (Eds.), *Activating theory: Lesbian, gay, bisexual politics*. London: Lawrence & Wishart.

Rich, A. (1980). Compulsory heterosexuality and lesbian existence. *Signs: Journal of Women in Culture and Society 5.4*, 31-60.

Rodgerson, G. (2000, June). I'm so very free. *Diva, 29*.

Rust, P.C. (1992). Who are we and where do we go from here? Conceptualizing bisexuality. In E.R. Weise (Ed.), *Closer to home: Bisexuality and feminism*. Seattle: Seal Press.

Shildrick, M., & Price, J. (1999). Breaking the boundaries of the broken body. In J. Price & M. Shildrick (Eds.), *Feminist theory and the body: A reader* (pp. 432-444). Edinburgh: Edinburgh University Press.

Showalter, E. (1986). Feminist criticism in the wilderness. In E. Showalter (Ed.), *The new feminist criticism: Essays on women, literature and theory* (pp. 234-270). London: Virago.

Sykes, G., & Matza, D. (1957). Techniques of neutralization. *American Sociological Review 22*, 664-670. Cited in A. Ault (1996). Hegemonic discourse in an oppositional community: Lesbian feminist stigmatization of bisexual women. In B. Beemyn & M. Eliason (Eds.), *Queer studies: A lesbian, gay, bisexual and transgender anthology*. New York: New York University Press.

_____A threat to women's freedom. (2000). Behind the mask website. <www.mask.org.za/sections/women/index.html>.

Viner, K. (2000, October 20-26). Alias Atwood. *Mail & Guardian*, pp. 34-35.

Welch, L. (2000, June/July). Tsitsi Tiripano. *Ms 10.4*, 12.

"Outside Belonging":
Multi-Sexual Relationships as Border Existence

Maria Pallotta-Chiarolli
Sara Lubowitz

[Haworth co-indexing entry note]: " 'Outside Belonging': Multi-Sexual Relationships as Border Exis-tence." Palotta-Chiarolli, Maria, and Sara Lubowitz. Co-published simultaneously in *Journal of Bisexuality* (Harrington Park Press, an imprint of The Haworth Press, Inc.) Vol. 3, No. 1, 2003, pp. 53-85; and: *Women and Bisexuality: A Global Perspective* (ed: Serena Anderlini-D'Onofrio) Harrington Park Press, an imprint of The Haworth Press, Inc., 2003, pp. 53-85. Single or multiple copies of this article are available for a fee from The Haworth Document Delivery Service [1-800-HAWORTH, 9:00 a.m. - 5:00 p.m. (EST). E-mail address: docdelivery@haworthpress.com].

SUMMARY. This article draws from an ongoing Australian research project with over 60 culturally and sexually diverse women in monogamous, open, and polyamorous relationships with bisexual-identifying and/or bisexual-behaving men. Positioned within a queer feminist deconstructive theoretical framework, this research provides insights into the border existences of these women and their partners, and their negotiations of "new rules" and boundaries in order to construct healthy relationships. What are the various ways that HIV/AIDS impacts women in relationships with bisexual men? How do they deal with issues such as social, community, workplace and familial ostracism? Probyn's term, "outside belonging" (1996: 9) is applicable to the border existences of these women and their bisexual male partners. Their multi-sexual relationships are both "outside" gendernormative and heteronormative constructs of marital and defacto relationships and yet "belonging," for the partners may "pass" as a "normal" couple. They are also "outside" the dominant constructs of Australian gay identity and community while simultaneously "belonging" due to their partners', and sometimes their own, same-sex attractions and relationships. *[Article copies available for a fee from The Haworth Document Delivery Service: 1-800-HAWORTH. E-mail address: <docdelivery@haworthpress.com> Website: <http://www.HaworthPress.com> © 2003 by The Haworth Press, Inc. All rights reserved.]*

KEYWORDS. Bisexuality, heterosexuality, gender and power, ethnic women, women's health, HIV/AIDS, monogamy, polyamory, trust/betrayal, relationships, marriage

"WHERE ARE WE? HOW DO WE?"

The women you will meet in this article are part of a larger ongoing Australian qualitative research project with over 60 women. Of diverse sexualities, ages and cultural backgrounds, the women are in monogamous, open and polyamorous marital and defacto relationships with bisexual-identifying and/or bisexual-behaving men. Positioned within a queer feminist deconstructive theoretical framework and analysis, this research will provide insights into the lived experiences and negotiated sexual, emotional and mental health strategies of sexually diverse women and the bisexually active men they are in marital and de facto relationships with. How do these relationships work? How do the men and women in these borderland relationships negotiate and establish "new rules" and boundaries in order to construct and maintain healthy sexual, emotional and social relationships? How do they deal with issues such as social, community, workplace and familial ostracism or the silence about their relationships within these networks?

We are compiling a collection of personal narratives, framed by theoretical analysis, for publication. These narratives are reconstructed from in-depth semi-structured interviews with women, which took place mainly in women's homes, in parks and workplaces. The women participated enthusiastically with the hope that their stories would be of use to other women in breaking the silence, revealing their diverse realities of "outside belonging" (Probyn, 1996), and thus assist others in similar relationships who are experiencing ostracism, isolation, misrepresentation or invisibility in wider societal, community and familial relationships and institutions. The personal narrative method was seen as accessible by the women who wanted their lives to be "written up" in ways that many people could read and engage with.

Narrative reconstruction of interview data is a long-established feminist research method (Acker et al., 1983). It is based on participant-researcher collaborations that provide vehicles for stories to be shared, discoveries made, and networks established. It is based on the concerns, needs, abilities, perspectives and recommendations of the participants (standpoint epistemology); and is empowering for the participant (participant as agent) (Brew, 1998; Denzin, 1997; Higgs, 1997; Connelly & Clandinin, 1990). It allows for the unsilencing of secrets without harming lives. It also provides an empowering impetus and a growing confidence among research participants to continue to find ways of being agents in the negotiation of the tensions surrounding the issues of stigma and shame in their lives, and to challenge the silence and denial regarding their locations within the wider society and their communities of significant others (McLaughlin & Tierney, 1993; Game & Metcalfe, 1996). Finally, narrative reconstruction makes the data accessible to a wider readership, and is more acceptable and comfortable to ethnic communities whose oral traditions involve the use of storytelling as a form of education (Anzaldua, 1987). The data then becomes a useful health promotion resource to be used within health services, community services and educational settings.

Within an Australian context, the relationships, lifestyles and health issues of women in relationships with bisexually active men are subjected to one or more of four types of problematic representations in sexual and emotional health research, and the populist culture. First, *underrepresentation* invisibilises these relationships. For example, very rarely do we read positive stories about a bisexually active man's strategies of negotiating his sexual practices with his female and male partners (Joseph, 1997; Hood et al., 1994). Second, *misrepresentation* occurs via media and popular culture stereotypical constructions, societal presumptions and prejudices. For example, "Bisexual Men as AIDS carriers" has been a dominant misrepresentation as well as: that all bisexually active men engage in secret sexual relations with men; that all bisexually active men identify as bisexual rather than heterosexual or gay; that all women in relationships with bisexually active men are unaware of or have no say in their partner's sexual identity and sexual practices (Richters, Lubowitz et al., 1997, 1999). Third, *outdated representation* is also evident. For example, people's polyamorous and multi-sexual relationship negotiations and partnering preferences lack current scholarship (Pallotta-Chiarolli, 1995a, 1995b, 1999; Alley, 1995). Finally, *homogenised representation* is also apparent where the diversity within groups, subcultures and categories such as sexual categories is not presented. For example, very rarely do we read of class, ethnicity, geographical location, gendered expectations and other factors that impact upon a woman's decisions and experiences in regard to being in a relationship with a bisexually active man (Pallotta-Chiarolli, 1995a, 1995b, 1995c, 1999).

Research undertaken by the Sydney Women and Sexual Health Survey (SWASH) by Richters, Lubowitz et al. (1997, 1999) produced evidence that gay identifying men had sex with women who identified as either lesbian or heterosexual. Of 585 women who completed the survey in 1996, 26% said they had sex with a gay- or bisexual-identifying man. In 1998, of the 554 women who completed the survey, 27% (212 women) said they had sex with a gay- or bisexual-identifying man. There is no Australian research or material on the broader issues framing sexual activity such as emotional relationships, marriage, age and child- rearing. There is also minimal cross-cultural material on these issues, although the need for this material is constantly raised by many services such as those that participated in the national audit and documented in the Commonwealth Department of Health and Family Services Report *Cultural Diversity and Men Who Have Sex With Men* (Pallotta- Chiarolli, 1998). For example, Lubowitz, in her role as co-ordinator of the Women of Bisexual Partners Network reported that 16 out of 100 women on her mailing list were of ethnic minority background and mostly married to ethnic minority bisexually active men (in Pallotta-Chiarolli, 1998: 11; see also Lubowitz, 1995a, 1995b, 1997, 1998).

"WHICH TRUTH? WHOSE REALITY?"

Women and men of diverse sexualities in marital and defacto relationships exist and belong inside/outside/on the borders of multiple binarily-constructed worlds. Foucault's construct of heterotopia acknowledges the notion of several different spaces and constructs co-existing and blurring within one space, as in the multiple-within space of a multi-sexual marriage (Foucault, 1986; Probyn, 1996). Probyn's term, "outside belonging," tries to describe the notion of movement "inbetween categories of specificity" (1996: 9) and is applicable to the women in our research and their bisexual male partners who see themselves as both "outside" gendernormative and heteronormative constructs of marital and defacto relationships and yet "belonging" in the sense that they are in a heterosexual relationships and may "pass" as a "normal" couple. They are also "outside" the dominant constructs of gay identity and gay community in Australia with its common marginalizing of nonlesbian identifying women and bisexual men while simultaneously "belonging" due to their partner's and sometimes their own same-sex attractions and relationships.

> Living as we did–on the edge–we developed a particular way of seeing reality. We looked both from the outside in and from the inside out. We focused our attention on the center as well as on the margin. (hooks in Trinh, 1990: 341)

Our research explores the interweaving within, between and beyond dichotomous logics, borders and boundaries that push all relationships, identities and communities into bifurcated categories. The women and their partners in our research inhabit locations within, between and beyond the binary hierarchy of lifelong marital monogamy and noncommitted, nonmonogamous sexual encounters; and the hierarchical duality of heterosexuality/homosexuality. Thus, our research interrogates "mainstream" hegemonic discourses of marriage, gender and sexuality and demonstrates how multi-sexual relationships "undo the logic and the clarity" of such constructs (Lionnet, 1989: 14). Our research makes visible and explores the not-so-orderly identities that underlie Identity, the realities that are lived within Reality, the truths that are concealed by The Truth. The problem is not that there is no truth, but that there is "too much truth" that powerful discourses conceal (Derrida, 1981: 105; see also Trinh, 1991). It is those borderzones of "too much truth," constructed as "unreal" or negated in dichotomous discursive boundaries, which will be explored.

One of the strategies adopted by long-term partners in response to this outsider-insider border positioning and external classification is the silencing of what those within the community of significant others and/or wider society consider "taboo" and "unreal": "The fact that reality is not always as discrete as we wish it were leads us not to reject our categories, but rather to reject reality" (Rust, 1992: 285). What becomes evident is how these multi-sexual relationships disrupt the constraints of the traditional heteronormative monogamous marital paradigm as well as acknowledging the knots and tangles that form and need to be unpicked due to ongoing constraints the paradigm places on them. For women in marital and de facto relationships with bisexual-identifying and/or bisexual-behaving men, sexual and gender identities and community allegiances are not fixed and dichotomous, but rather fluid, transitory, fragmented, episodic:

> But every place she went
> they pushed her to the other side
> and that other side pushed her to the other side
> of the other side of the other side
> Kept in the shadows of the other.
> (Trinh, 1990: 328)

Mestizaje or borderland theory seeks to define cultural identity as being in process, multi-placed and shifting (Anzaldua, 1987). Individuals locate themselves and are constructed by social, political and cultural forces as being mestizaje, meaning located within, outside, on the borders, or "slipping between the cracks" of social and cultural groups and established discourses. We found borderland theory to be a useful theoretical and analytical tool applicable to the multi-placement and inbetweennness many of the women experienced (some of whom were ethnic), because they were in multi-sexual relationships. Mestizaje persons find themselves often challenging and being challenged by the discourses and political ideologies of what is binarily constructed as the powerful centre such as the heterosexual monogamist marital "norm," and the power-challenging or excluded margins, such as the homosexual nonmarital "other" (Pallotta-Chiarolli, 1995a, 1996).

It needs to be remembered that this power-challenging homonormative margin is struggling with its own internal systems of inclusion and exclusion around bisexuality. Gay communities are also struggling with power disputes and structural tensions around debates such as lobbying for marital rights and whether these marriages should assimilate to heteronormative monogamist constructs or create broader options such as nonmonogamous and polyamorous marriages. Thus, we are not positioning homonormativity alongside heteronormativity in terms of power within the wider Australian society. Rather, we deconstruct difference and power within the nonheterosexual margin as a reflection and emulation of the workings of heteronormative and gendernormative discourses within the wider Australian society. The effects of homonormativity in relation to bisexuality and multi-sexual marriages are explored in our research as a reflection of the wider sociopolitical heteronormative need to neatly categorise and divide persons into either/or sexualities, genders and relationship models in order to control and manipulate. The success and power of these heteronormative systems of control and manipulation are evident in the internal exclusionary and divisive measures applied to bisexuality within gay and lesbian communities.

To deconstruct hierarchical opposition, such as heterosexual/homosexual, married/not married, monogamy/promiscuity as we do in our research is to undo and displace it, to situate it differently. We use deconstructionist tools that question and bend frames that set up boundaries (see Derrida, 1976, 1978, 1979, 1981). There is a need to investigate the actual boundary, fence, interval, gap, itself, thereby exploring the inbetween, the within, and the mixtures inherent in this borderzone where the women see their relationships as situated. There is a need to deconstruct heteronormativity and homonormativity in order to make visible the existence of bisexual identities and multi-sexual relationships consisting of unclassifiability, impurity, hybridity, fluidity, which manage to survive if not thrive on diversity, multiplicity and ambiguity, even as they are constrained by panopticonic sociocultural and political surveillance and regulation.

In order to understand and deconstruct the borderland locations of women in multi-sexual relationships with bisexual-identifying and/or bisexual-behaving men, we examine the very processes of positioning. Our research reveals the significance of three interwoven forces of sociopolitical structure and power: social ascription being the labels and categories (both affirming and negating) imposed on the women and their partners by the sites of power in the wider society such as the law, education, religion and medical institutions; *community acknowledgment* being the labels and categories one's significant others such as members of ethnic and gay communities affirm or disapprove of; and *personal agency* being the individual woman and her partner selecting and determining necessary or desired labels from the constructions available, or attempting to devise an alternative relationship model for themselves.

The following narrative will take us into the border existence "outside belonging" relationship of Alice and her partner Paul in order to illustrate the interwoven machinations of these three forces.

I'm sitting on a bench after a jog in Hyde Park, Sydney, just diagonally across from the beginning of Oxford Street, the heart of "gay Sydney," when an elderly couple, arm in arm, sit next to me, she in tweed skirt, he in tweed jacket, smiling in bemusement at my flushed sweaty face. They're taking a break from their daily walk, they explain, before heading home.

Where's home, I want to know, thinking that means some major bus-trip or train-ride to a leafy outer suburb.

No. They nod toward Oxford Street. Home is a twelfth floor "tiny unit, dear" in Darlinghurst. "We gave away the garden and the big house in the suburbs years ago, much to the dismay of our conservative thirty-something children," Alice explains, her smile an engaging mix of grandmotherly affection and grand dame confidence.

"Most of our friends live around here and why have a garden when you can have a whole park?" Paul adds, his slim, tanned, wrinkled arm, a silver bracelet around his wrist, making a graceful semi-circle in the air around him.

We get to talking about exercise and aging, and then about families, and then about love, and then about sexualities, and then about Mardi Gras and bi-phobia, and then about their marriage, and then Alice and I agree to meet there again the next day.

While the breeze plays on her carefully styled bob grey hair and the dappled sunlight catches her shiny blue eyes in the wrinkled but carefully made up face, Alice talks and laughs and gently pats me as if imparting the wisdom of age.

Alice is seventy-two, Paul seventy-four. They have lived together for almost all of their forty-eight married years. Throughout most of those years, Paul was openly having relationships with men. "But he's always loved me and I've always loved him, and only him. We have three children. Well, they're adults now, a bit stodgy really, including one of my daughters who's a lesbian. Being grandparents is just marvellous. So, there's that whole family thing, which Paul and I truly wanted to have together. And yes, he did have very important relationships with men along the way, and yes, there were times I worried he'd leave me and then I'd tell myself he'd be a fool to do so, and I was far from going to be dependent, financially or otherwise, on a man. I'm very radical I guess although people look at me and see a little old lady in a North Shore cardigan and tweed skirt and support hose, and think I'd be so homophobic and subjugated and one of Fred Nile's props." She laughs and looks proud, strong and confident as she continues, her eyes peering down the length of Oxford Street. *"Long ago, I even told him that if ever he should wish to move out and live with a man and see me and the children as well, I could live with that, as long as he did his fair share of parenting and equal financial supporting. But it never happened for longer than a month or so."* She leans forward with a mischievous smile. *"For the last few months, he's actually been spending some nights with another old gentleman but he calls me every morning and we arrange a good old-fashioned date, usually strolling around here or having lunch, depending on when I'm available, what with my commitments with senior women's groups, some volunteer work in Legal Aid, and some volunteer work at the hospice with AIDS patients and women with cancer. Over forty years on, and we're still arranging dates and rendezvous. I have always got to know his male lovers as friends. That helps break down any misconceptions or illusions they may have that I'm either dumb or insignificant.*

I think our children hover between accepting us and being quite envious of the special love we have for each other, especially my son who's heading for a divorce if he doesn't smarten up, and bewilderment that we're too old now for that "free love" sixties hippy thing, which Paul and I did for awhile and they would have had around them as children. But they're a little too caught in all this hoo-hah about having a clean and clearcut sexual identity, and it being one of two alternatives, heterosexual or homosexual. Even my daughter, who loves women, has confined herself into being a lesbian and behaving as if it's a uniform, or what do they say these days, a fashion statement, rather than a way of loving."

Having always felt I was born too late to enjoy that fabulous decade, I want to know about her as a hippy, about their lives in the sixties. Alice laughs scornfully and pats my hand again. "What I'm going to say may seem very old-fashioned but it was actually quite radical for those days and for the people in those circles we moved in. You see, I was monogamous all the way through, dear. That's the way I was and am. But I'm certainly not a doormat. I have always been very strong and independent. I had my own professional life as a lawyer. And try practicing law at a time when your own husband is carrying on in what were then ex-

tremely illegal pursuits, let alone being a woman lawyer. So I may have been heterosexual and monogamous in an era of polymorphous perversity but I was a feminist before feminism became a household word. I always demanded Paul's honesty, his love, his equal parenting and domestic work, and a good sexual, affectionate relationship. Actually, I think it was my feminism and the fact that I mixed with such boorish patriarchal oafs in my legal career that steered me into loving a man like Paul. He was a lawyer too, a rare male breed among legal men back then, still is, I think, when I look at the corporate emotional sterility of many men, and unfortunately some women, in the legal field today. He was sensitive, he treated me with gentleness, and he was always so much fun. And he's still quite debonair isn't he? How could you keep someone like that to yourself? Why would you want to? His bisexuality was one of the components that make him the man I fell deeply in love with when we were in our early twenties and there was no way I was going to leave him unless I was unhappy with him."

She looks so assured, so proud and comfortable, I have to dig deeper. "So you never had a doubt? You never wanted him all to yourself?"

"The eighties weren't so good." A frown has appeared and a slightly trembling hand rises to adjust the collar of her pastel blue cardigan as she again gazes down the length of Oxford Street. "Good between us, but very bad out there. The AIDS epidemic you know. We lost friends. We were terrified of losing each other." She turns to me and pats me again. "Now remember how you idealized the sixties? Well, it wasn't all peace, love and harmony. You've heard of how some women were delegated to serving cups of tea at anti-war demonstration meetings? Well, women were like endless cups of tea for some men. Women were often told free love was liberating them when in actual fact it often made them more enslaved, to be sexually accessible and available to even more men without any control in the matter. And of course, let's not even begin to talk about genital warts, herpes, and all those sexually transmitted diseases lots of girls ended up with. The pill was in, a woman's responsibility to relieve men of debilitating paternity, but condoms for "real men" were still out.

"So the eighties came along and made me feel relieved I had stayed monogamous and that Paul and I had done something quite radical in the sixties, insist on him using a condom with men. But all those rumors about the ways the virus was spread–toilet seats, mosquitoes, sweat–sounds like a description of your typical beat, doesn't it?

. And not only that but the way bisexual men became these sexual demons, "spreading disease with the greatest of ease" as that Mortein fly-

spray advert on TV used to say. So Paul became this demonic person that only a demented, dependent and naïve little lady like me would cling to."

She shifts indignantly on the bench and I can see that that certainly wasn't Alice. She regains a dignified composure and continues, "So sexual ownership was something I contemplated only for a few months in that state of total fear of whether what Paul and I had always practised, what became fashionably known as 'safe sex,' was really enough against this 'Gay Men's Disease.' Especially after one of Paul's long-term intimate friends and very dear, dear man whose wife never knew until he was hospitalized, died in the Sacred Heart Hospice, abandoned by his family and most of his friends, straight and gay. Dreadful, dreadful tragedy for all involved."

Alice looks away again in the direction of the Hospice. "But overall, the hardest part of our marriage was the secrecy we had to keep for years and years with work colleagues and family, and the agonies and hurts we caused and had to face when some loved ones found out along the way. But as we got older we got tougher and braver. That's one of the many good things about aging, you know. You stop worrying about being judged. You get freer. And along the way, we've got stronger as we've watched other so-called 'normal, natural' marriages crumble or just dry up, especially the relationships of some of our knockers. And we got stronger in standing up to these gay activist types who couldn't figure out why he didn't leave me and lead a 'normal' gay life. Come to think of it, that word 'normal' gets used by everyone to knock someone else!"

We see Paul navigating his way carefully across the intersection of Oxford and College Streets, a smiling old man, wispy silver hair lifting in the breeze, slowly and surely making his way while the younger studs rush by. As he ambles along the path, he spots Alice and breaks into a smile far too delighted and far too child-like to be a performance. His braceleted wrist comes up in a wave to her, the sun glinting on the silver. She makes room for him on the bench next to her and pats it, takes his elbow and helps him sit, then kisses him lightly, leaving a smudge of pink lipstick like an extra blush on his cheek, and then comments on the lovely cologne he's wearing. He was at his lover's house last night and she hasn't seen him since yesterday lunchtime. But later today they're being picked up by the lesbian daughter who will whisk them away for a few days in the Blue Mountains where they will "indulge in long walks, long lunches, long naps and long sex sessions," Paul informs me while Alice shoves him playfully.

*As they stroll carefully away, arm in arm, back toward Oxford Street,
its shiny flags, shiny cars and shiny people shimmering in the sun, I'm
left with one of Alice's phrases shimmering inside her own heart:
"That's love, really. Wanting the best for someone you love. Even if
means breaking all the rules of what love is meant to be."*

In the rest of this paper, we will explore the previously outlined three
forces separately and in greater detail, using specific narratives based
on interviews with women to illustrate their workings and constraints.

"THEY SAY, THEREFORE, I SHOULD BE": BORDERING THE WIDER SOCIETY

Social ascription refers to the labels and classifications imposed on
one by the powerful central discourses within a society as upheld by institutions such as religion, education and the law:

> The barracks stands by the church stands by the schoolroom . . .
> surveillance depends [upon them] for its strategies of objectifi-
> cation, normalization and discipline.

(Bhabha, 1990: 86)

Women in multi-sexual relationships in our research are particularly
aware of how their multiple realities are subjected to scissoring, simpli-
fying and homogenizing by "this ready-made code and having to accommodate oneself to it" (Trinh, 1991: 136). Mason calls this wider
societal code regarding relationships and sexuality the "discourse of silence" that renders multi-sexual relationships "both unseeable and un-
knowable" (1995: 87). From within a paradigm of dichotomous logics
enforced through medical and other institutions, women in relationships with gay or bisexual men feel that there are only two contradictory, equally persuasive, either/or ways of viewing their multi-sexual
partnerships. For example, is their willingness to accept an open sexual
contract flexibility or passivity? Is their refusal assertiveness or rigidity? What signifies self-esteem and what signifies a lack of self-esteem?
Are they really unhappy with their partners or are they told by a wider
society that they should be, and if they aren't, is there something "devi-
ant" about them as women? Gochros refers to this either/or conflict as
"cognitive dissonance, defined here as the disparity between old ideals

and new realities" without alternatives and outlets that would assist women in navigating and interrogating their way through, between and within these limited polar presumptions (1985: 110).

Gochros also refers to two syndromes that may arise out of this either/or dissonance: "*male chauvinism* and *liberation ethics*." In some multi-sexual relationships, husbands claim as their right, as a man or an oppressed minority, to do anything they please and that it is the wife's duty, as a woman or a symbolic oppressor, to help him "cheerfully" (1985: 110). Several women in our research did discuss the gendered oppression they experienced in relationships that were coercive and inequitable. For the women in mentally and emotionally abusive relationships, the sexuality of their partners was problematic not so much because it was nonheterosexual but because they had not known or had no opportunity to consider their options before entering into the relationship. It was as if the ground had shifted under them: the socially approved and "known" marriage they had entered into had become "unknown" territory to be mapped out again. Some women said the sexuality of their partners was less significant than the way the men upheld and performed traditional and hegemonic constructs of masculinity.

The sexual and emotional health consequences of dominant social constructs are evident in the following narrative where a multi-sexual couple find their lives bordering presence and absence, invisibility and reality, Truth and truths, exteriors and interiors, belonging and being on the outside.

It's a green leafy suburb of Sydney, one of the white Anglo established areas. It screams money at you–but with subtlety. The kind of suburb where every house has off-street parking for the imported luxury cars. It's so quiet except for the birds singing in the large native gum trees.

It's such a warm, sunny spring day as we have fresh coffee and caramel slice, and start to chat. Her husband is in the garden out of sight and ear shot. He has been told to stay there until we have finished. Elizabeth starts explaining their lives, their 30 years of marriage. He was a successful business man for many many years and money has never been a problem.

On the Outside, the "perfect" white affluent Australian family. Two children. Nice house.

On the Inside, he's been having sex with men for 30 years and has kept it a secret all that time.

He says he's bisexual but has never had sex with any other woman because that would be a betrayal of the marriage. He told her he was having sex with men after he told her he was HIV+. She was told all this life-altering information in 10 minutes. It was too much to bear. She began to care for him even though part of her hated him, for the betrayal and hurt that she felt. This isn't how it was meant to be, not in this suburb, not in this kind of family.

A year later while still coming to terms with it all and trying to work out what she thinks and feels about her future, she is diagnosed with breast cancer. The roles reverse and now he cares for her.

Elizabeth starts to explain what attracted her to him at the start. "I was only in my early twenties. In fact I think I might have been twenty when I first met him, but I had had a lot of boyfriends, and the thing that appealed to me was I found him sexier than the other blokes that I'd been out with, actually."

So I ask, "And do you know what that 'sexiness' was?"

"I don't know. I suppose his gentle approach to things. He was kinder and had a soft side to him, which a lot of the other fellows didn't have."

"Did he seem to be a bit more in touch with some of his emotions?"

Elizabeth's answer takes me by surprise "Yes, or more in touch with my emotions."

So how did Elizabeth find out that her husband was having sex with men? "We went away for a few days in January, in the school holidays, and we came back and he said he wasn't feeling awfully well. He got very sick and we thought it was flu. He had a very bad cough and a very high temperature. So, I moved into the other bedroom, and played the dutiful wife-cum-nurse maid and was waiting on him hand and foot, and had the doctor over to see him twice. The doctor said he thought it was probably a very bad dose of flu, but he'd get him tested for a few other strange viral diseases that were around like Ross River Fever, and those sorts of things.

And after about two weeks of being very sick, he started to get better and on the Sunday morning, the 31st of January, he said would I come and sit next to him on the bed. I did. I said, "Oh, you're not joking, Oh, this looks really serious. What's this about?" And he said, "Oh, yes, it is serious. I have to tell you I know what I've got." I said, "What do you mean what you've got?" He said, "What sickness I've got." He said, "I've got HIV".

I was totally stunned, of course. My next question was "How did you get it?" So, then it came out, but it came out in short bursts. He led me to believe at that stage that this had only been going on since he lost his job. I really got terribly upset and depressed and went to see my GP, and I was almost suicidal at that stage, because I thought we had a really good marriage. We had this sort of relationship where we'd always done things together, but we'd also always done things individually. I mean, I go out to dinner with friends and he goes to concerts and theatre with friends if I'm not interested, and that's been fine, because it's always been a very trusting relationship. I've traveled overseas by myself. He's traveled overseas by himself. I thought it was all above-board and it was all fine. But, it obviously wasn't. The first thing I had to do was to go and have an AIDS test."

I have to ask, "And how did that make you feel?" I want to know what a woman who most probably has never imagined herself in the situation of being tested for HIV would feel.

"Oh, I felt absolutely awful. I really felt demoralised and demeaned, and he took me along to see his doctor because he'd been going to a clinic in Darlinghurst and having regular tests. It also made me terribly, terribly angry because I'd realised that we'd never had safe sex. So, for years he'd been putting my life at risk, and so for all the, "I really love you's" and whatever he said to me, "You're the only person I care for" I think, "Yeah, but you care for yourself more, because you weren't prepared to be totally responsible all the time." And, he answers that with, "Well, everybody behaves irrational at times." Most of the time he had safe sex. Just every so often, he didn't and he now blames the counsellors at the clinic he was going to because they failed. They couldn't tell him what to do to stop having unsafe sex. I said, "You cannot blame other people." "Oh, no, I don't blame them entirely" is the reply, but they get the blame for his lack of responsibility. But, the anger that I feel about that issue will, I don't think, ever go away. I think if you love somebody enough, you don't put their lives on the line. It's bad enough to put your own life on the line, but to put somebody else's life on the line. And just going into the clinic and having to be tested for AIDS by doctors who, I must say, were always very lovely, but I'd never seen them before. And the clientele at the clinic were different. Some of them obviously did not just have HIV but had AIDS, judging by the look of them. I mean, they looked very, very ill. So, I was exposed to a whole different scene there, too."

Thus, many women in our research feel anger and resentment at the dominant assumptions and presumptions that construct the triad of marriage, monogamy and heterosexuality as unquestioned and unquestionable. This has rendered them ignorant, vulnerable, powerless and unable to make informed choices and decisions about their lives and health. Having found themselves immersed in a situation that they had no discursive framework for at the beginning of their relationships, lacking knowledge, open communication and exposure to both viable possibilities and dangers, they are calling for sociocultural and political visibility in health and education structures, and in popular culture. They call for the broadening of limited discursive frameworks within which their relationships are either rendered invisible or misrepresented, and/or within which they find themselves lacking agency and control.

> All sides of the issue need to be considered in the media, research, social theory, and religious thought . . . we need: social realists to affirm society's need for stability by exploring alternative marriage and family arrangements and sexual realists to point out the diversity of sexual orientations as part of the natural order and but one aspect of the individuals who make up society. (Buxton, 1991: 275)

"THEY SAY, THEREFORE, I MUST BE": BORDERING THE COMMUNITY

In a racist, sexist and heteronormative society that has despised and devalued certain groups, it is necessary and desirable for members of those groups to adhere with one another and celebrate a common culture, heritage, and experience. This grouping is usually referred to as a "community" such as in ethnic, religious and gay communities. For example, the transition from being homosexual to being gay is seen as "enculturation" into a "gay community," involving the "learning of a lot of social skills" in the "homosexualization" of life (Dowsett, 1997: 162-163). Part of this learning can be problematic as individuals negotiate the identities with which they have come into the community, deciding what needs to be shed and what needs to adopted:

> not only do poofs and dykes come out, we also come IN to the gay community, and this can be just as harrowing as coming out to the rest of the world . . . a coming into the gay scene can be accompanied with a fair bit of angst and a frenzied attempt at repackaging ourselves (Smart, 1994: 9).

Thus, identity politics and the communities they represent struggle with the need for labels around which to call for civil rights. Simultaneously, they are developing discourses and institutions for bringing differently identified groups and individuals together without suppressing or subsuming the differences within (Epstein, 1987). In its drive to invert the hierarchical privilege of powerful dominant groups, a particular marginal group may inherit the symbolic terms of hierarchy and becomes a place of production of new hierarchies. Thus, ethnic migrant communities may strive for cohesion, success and traditional cultural maintenance in a new country by policing and regulating sexuality and marriage, particularly in relation to women. Family and community become prime sites for cultural and religious regulation against a mainstream world that threatens to dilute the values and traditions of the homeland (Pallotta-Chiarolli, 1995c, 1998, 1999).

The "multiple within" realities of mestizaje such as women in multisexual relationships negotiating ethnic, religious and familial gendernormative and heteronormative constructs while seeking another community for social and emotional networking and support call for the following questions to be addressed: how does one use the word "community" without meaning homogeneity; and where and how are the boundaries of exclusion and inclusion of a community drawn? How do we work with ethnic communities, gay communities and women's health services in order to construct spaces for women in multi-sexual relationships to negotiate their multiple-within realities and decisions? As Giroux writes, identity politics

> enabled many formerly silenced and displaced groups to emerge from the margins of power and dominant culture to reassert and reclaim suppressed identities and experiences; but in doing so, they often substituted one master narrative for another, invoked a politics of separatism, and suppressed differences within their own "liberatory" narratives. (1993: 3)

More of the following examples need to be made visible to the wider society as well as to specific ethnic and sexual communities with fixed heteronormative monogamist codes and regulations in relation to family and monosexuality.

I was greeted at the door of a small neat house in a lower socioeconomic outer suburb of Melbourne by Soulla's husband, Keith. I had never met him but had heard from Soulla, a Greek migrant, that he was

*"just wonderful." He was now very calm but his eyes revealed the ag-
ony he was going through. "I just love her so much, you know? I'm trying to keep myself together for her sake but it's really hard." He took me
to the bedroom and I sat on the bed holding Soulla's frail hand. After
awhile, Keith brought us cups of tea and Greek biscuits, then Soulla
asked him if he could leave her alone with me for awhile.*

*Soulla looked urgently at me, squeezing my hand tightly. "I haven't
got long and I want to tell you because I have not told anyone in my
community and family and I want you to know about me so you can tell
other Greeks and Italians that these things do happen and it is too much
for us to have to bear these crosses in silence." I look over to a
gold-leafed crucifix on her bedside table.*

*Soulla had migrated from Greece with her family in her early teens.
She met Keith while working in a factory. From the beginning she loved
him because "he was not rough and never laughed at my poor English,
my funny clothes, the way I knew nothing about sex and was so shy" and
seemed to respect the expectations her culture had of her as a young
woman. Thus, he agreed to chaperoned outings, a quick traditional
Greek wedding, and allowing his two daughters to be raised in the Greek
Orthodox Church. After a few years of marriage, he became depressed
for months and then finally admitted that although he loved Soulla, he
could no longer hide from her or from himself the fact that he was also attracted to and having sex with men. His own Catholic priest had told him
that by marrying Soulla these feelings would go away. That was definitely
wrong but the priest had been right that a woman brought up so inno-
cently and ignorantly as a "good Greek girl" in a Greek community
would never suspect that he was also attracted to men.*

*But now he had fallen in love with a man he wanted to see regularly but
he would be devastated if Soulla left him or took the children away from
him.*

*"He was always such a good father, doing everything for them. He
never treated me like a slave. I had already had to fight very hard to be
allowed to marry him because he wasn't Greek and my father had
warned me that Australian men couldn't be trusted and if he ever did
anything to shame and dishonour the family, it would be my responsibility as a woman to keep the marriage together. If anything went
wrong, my father threatened to kill him and me." Soulla's eyes fill
with tears. She speaks slowly. "I remember the next few years after
Keith telling me being those of great anger and frustration. We each
tried to commit suicide at separate times. My religious background
also prevented me from ending the marriage, from going public be-*

cause of the shame it would bring to my family and my daughters who would be shunned later when it was their turn to marry. And Keith, poor Keith, felt so trapped and so bad having caused so much pain to me, the woman he loved. Because I know he did love me. With time, the pain began to ease. There was too much love between us and the love for our daughters and all the hard work to get above our working-class backgrounds. We couldn't get divorced. It would've killed us even if my father hadn't carried out his threats. Our daughters are adolescents now, young women, and they love their father so much. They know about him."

I have to ask, "If you knew then what you know now . . ."

Soulla smiles wearily. "Would I have married him? I don't know. Once he entered my parents' home I had to marry him. There was no alternative. I was spoiled goods. And yes, if I hadn't married him, I would've missed such a wonderful husband. Compared to the many married Greek men I know and hear about who beat their wives or drink or gamble or run around with women, there is no way I would give him up without losing so much. He is a wonderful husband and father and my best friend. Other women envy me because he is just so caring. And if they knew the truth, they'd spit at him. It's so stupid. But I would have done the same once. My religious faith has also sustained me in knowing there is a reason for everything." Soulla placed a hand on where a breast should've been. "I cannot leave this bed now. Two years I've been fighting cancer and I know why God sent him to me. The love, dedication and care he has given me is the answer. Knowing that when I die, the girls are in good hands."

Soulla leans forward to me. "Don't tell my family all this. They may stop him from raising our daughters, or may not help him. It is enough what he has gone through and what he'll go through. He has a boyfriend, four years now, who is supporting him as he cares for me. He needs that support. It was hard to find such a man because the gay community doesn't like men like Keith. I'm glad he won't be alone when I'm gone."

Many women partners of gay and bisexual men in our research are calling for political and social awareness and action, and health promotion campaigns in ethnic, gay and other communities such as the women's movement. They become aware of the "double-barreled stigma of homophobia and sex-role stereotyping" as well as ethnocentrism as barriers they and their partners face both within and outside their communities of significant others (Gochros, 1989: 137).

"I SAY, THEREFORE, I AM":
PERSONAL AGENCY AND STRATEGIES FOR THRIVING ON THE BORDER

I did it, and I didn't die. I didn't even languish. Quite the contrary–
I flourished. And with every fresh act of daring against the taboo, I
blossomed more. Instead of hiding all scrunched up in my fearful
skin, clinging to it, I began to slough it off and stand up straight,
clear and clean, my strong new skin gleaming in the sunlight.
(Johnson, 1987: 9)

Whether they be within the wider society or within a minority community, constructions of social relations with no room for personal agency
but only for "social puppets on fine, flexible wires dancing across stages
not of their own making" are problematic (Boden, 1990: 193). People
are, and always have been, active agents in the constitution of their un-
folding social and personal worlds (Davis, 1991; Butler, 1993).
Mestizaje borderland theory states that within these regulatory and silencing structural and discursive frameworks and panopticonic processes can be found some degree of agency (Anzaldua, 1987; Sewell,
1992; Molina, 1994; Lugones, 1994). The types of resources to which
agents have access and the knowledgeable skills involved in the practices they perform, as well as their discursive knowledge of broader social conditions, always exist within determinate historical and spatial
bounds. However, if agents were unable to originate new forms of activity then "it would be impossible to account for the extraordinary variation in social conduct that has been exhibited in the course of human
history"(Cohen, 1987: 291).

There are particular circumstances that tend to influence the level
and nature of agency of women with bisexually active male partners.
What they need includes the following: access to knowledge of their social, gendered and sexual locations, including health promotion programs, textual resources and resource persons; the modes, economic or
otherwise, of articulating and utilising this knowledge; and the means of
disseminating this knowledge to others such as their support networks,
their children, co-workers, and others who validate and respect their
knowledge. The women in our research believe that if enough people or
even a few people who are powerful enough act in innovative ways to
break down invisibility and discrimination, their action may have the
consequence of being gradually transformative, at individual, interpersonal, cultural and institutional levels.

> Freedom grows in the cracks. People create options, choices, alternatives for themselves. (McGregor, 1980: 313)

The women unanimously stated that their voluntary participation in this research and their desire to see it published and accessible is an act of agency, social and political action, a strategy for connecting across silences and generating visibility and knowledge.

Several women in our research acknowledge that the very act of living while constantly interrogating and evaluating one's borderland multi-sexual relationship is an act of resistant agency:

> Curdle-separation is not something that happens to us but something we do . . . code-switching; categorical blurring and confusion; . . . caricaturing of the fragmented selves we are in our groups; revealing the chaotic in production; . . . undermining the orderliness of the social ordering; marking our cultural mixtures as we move; . . . Thus curdled behavior is not only creative but also constitutes itself as a social commentary, . . . an act of social creative defiance. (Lugones, 1994: 478)

This kind of border existence opens up space for experimentation; reality is confronted with liberty and possibility. The self must

> put itself to the test of reality, . . . both to grasp the points where change is possible and desirable, and to determine the precise form this change should take. (Foucault, 1984: 46)

Our research finds that most women and their partners pretend to the outside world to live conventional heteronormative monogamous lives. "It's safer to appear to be just like everything else. We can't know how many secrets exist behind the appearances" (Whitney, 1990: 227). The concept of the closet as an agentic strategy is discussed by many border-dwelling women in our research, reflecting the words of Aruna, a lesbian of Tamil and Malaysian backgrounds dealing with the triad of sexism, racism and homophobia impacting on her life:

> Even as I am suspended between borders, between definitions, . . . I survive by remembering that going in and out of closets is a strategy for working to remove the conditions that make my closets necessary in the first place. (1994: 374)

The closet represents a possible mode of evading "other more undesirable forms of governance" such as rigidly being hung up on what we metaphorically call the clothesline to be buffeted by wind and rain and heat, and it is used in order to "assert a degree of control" over life (Mason, 1995: 87).

Our research has also revealed that many women who identify as heterosexual, bisexual or lesbian are deliberately choosing gay-identifying or bisexual-identifying men as partners, hence deliberately choosing to enter the borderland of ambiguity and unclassifiability (see Pallotta-Chiarolli, 1995a, 1996; Whitney, 1990).

> They bring the outside into the inside, and poison the comfort of order with suspicion of chaos . . . They are that third element which should not be. The true hybrids, the monsters: not just unclassified, but unclassifiable . . . they question oppositions as such, the very principle of the opposition, the plausibility of dichotomy . . . They unmask the brittle artificiality of division. (Bauman, 1990: 146, 148-149)

In every case, with issues such as monogamy, living together, having other same-sex or opposite-sex partners, the bottom line seems to be choice and agency:

> In a sense, they are the reluctant pioneers of a different family form, and by living the way they do, they are making a statement about the nature of love and commitment. (Whitney, 1990: 107)

As Gochros' research and ours illustrates, there are women who expect gender equality and interpersonal connectedness in multi-sexual relationships, and will not settle for anything less:

> [she] rated herself (and appeared) highly self-confident and assertive, . . . [and there] seemed to be an emphasis on non-sexism in choice of mate. (Gochros, 1989: 40)

Some women in our research linked this desire for equitable, flexible and emotionally and sexually satisfying relationships with their actively looking for bisexual or gay men as partners. They believed these men had interrogated hegemonic constructs of heterosexual masculinity and the interlinked traditional gendered expectations and assumptions of women. This supports Nahas and Turley's (1979) ground-breaking research into what they defined then as a "new couple," meaning the relationship between a heterosexual woman and a homosexual man where both wish this relationship to be the primary one in their lives, understood as either monogamous or nonmonogamous. Nahas and Tyler's research concludes that the women who are happy living in such a relationship have several things in common, which many of the women in our study had as well, including the bisexual and/or feminist and/or polyamorous women we interviewed. They appear to be women whose fulfillment in life does not depend on conventional notions of marriage and motherhood; who were not dependent on their partners for contentment in social and business affairs; who feel personally and professionally equal to men; and who do not consider monogamy to be a necessary ingredient for a successful relationship. These women are less concerned with "maintaining appearances and upholding tradition" than with "achieving one-to-one compatibility" and consider their relationship, "not as a poor compromise, but with enthusiasm and flexibility" (Nahas & Turley, 1979: 21-22). Hence, personal agency far outweighs the significance of social ascription and the approval of significant others.

Thus, the women in our research in emotionally and sexually fulfilling multi-sexual relationships speak about establishing rules and boundaries that are based on their relationship's needs and circumstances rather than on adhering to conventional rules regarding marriage and monogamy, gendernormativity and heteronormativity. These include: setting and negotiating the number of outside partners and the kinds of interactions allowed from monogamy to unlimited outside partners, and from casual one-off encounters to polyamory-parallel or interwoven sexual-emotional relationships; negotiating time allocation and energy management in regard to sharing and balancing work, childcare, home duties, social events together and apart, and sexual-emotional relationships together and apart; not lying about outside sexual activities and negotiating how much detail needs to be recounted; not picking someone up when partners go out together; not engaging in sex with others in the home they share; only engaging in threesomes together or sharing each other's partners; meeting any potential outside partners of one's partner on a social level at first and having the right to veto that relationship becoming sexual or more emotionally intimate; and strict negotiations around safer sex practices, ranging from a limitation on the kinds of sexual practices permitted with outside partners to organizing regular STI/HIV testing.

However, women tell us that agreed upon rules are not always followed and may cause conflict in relationships. Likewise, rules change over time to adapt to changing circumstances. Indeed, it appears that multi-sexual relationships often begin with numerous ground rules, but these decrease over time as they appear to fail, or as the partners become increasingly confident and trusting of each other, and/or if they are gradually considered too rigid or too oppressive (Weinberg, Williams & Pryor, 1994).

The following narrative illustrates the role of personal agency in negotiating a relationship's "outside belonging," which includes the strategic use of the closet.

I am sitting with Gloria on Gloria's back veranda in suburban Adelaide. We're eating the homemade tiramisu Gloria has brought out. "An entree before the barbie," she laughs. Gloria's husband, Sam, is swinging their kids on the clothesline inbetween cooking the meat on the barbecue. Both sets of Italian grandparents are in the garden discussing tomatoes, wine-making and basking in the satisfaction of sitting in the backyard of married children, knowing they have fulfilled their parental duties in getting their children to this stage of sistemazione. Gloria shrugs. "Sam and I are bisexual, we occasionally have other male and female lovers in ongoing relationships together or separately, we are very happily married, and we love being Italian and hope our children cherish their cultural heritage the way we do. But all these contradictions are not meant to exist. We're too queer for the queer."

She looks at the various members of her family enjoying the sunshine and peace. "From when Sam and I were teenagers, we knew we were different. Not only different but supposedly nonexistent. It's as if we were the only kids on the whole planet who were not gay and not straight, who wanted to have the good old-fashioned Italian wedding and raise an Italian family but not accept what would've been traps for us like needing to be monogamous and heterosexual. Well, we still feel like we're the only Italian-Australians that have ever been through this and it's so isolating sometimes. There's no one else to talk to, no one else to tell you your lives and mixed identities are realities, your sort of marriage exists. But every now and again, we wonder who else is living similar realities but also in absolute silence? We're real. We're flesh and blood. He's there cooking the barbie and playing with the kids and I'm here scoffing my face with tiramisu and our parents are there seeing what they want to see and not needing to know the rest. We're resigned to the fact that in our lifetime there won't be any public acknowledge-

ment of our particular situations. These days it's all about multicultural identity and gay identity and every now and again there's stuff about a multicultural gay identity, but neither the multiculturalists nor the gay activists are prepared to publicly discuss our complexities. But more of us will come out of the woodwork."

Gloria sighs and stretches out her arms to her world. "I love being married, I love being bisexual, I love being Italian-Australian. They can co-exist and they do right here in this suburban backyard."

Our research supports the pioneering research of Nahas and Turley (1979), Whitney (1990), Gochros (1985; 1989) and Buxton (1991; 2001) which calls for the need to insert knowledge and debates about these multi-sexual relationships into the public world of the wider society so that the personal agentic strengths and strategies deployed by many women and their partners is increasingly acknowledged, supported by wider cultural, structural and institutional frameworks such as in health, education and the law.

These couples were pioneers traveling uncharted trails without the companionship of the wagon train or the leadership of a wagonmaster. Given the handicaps they faced, what seems surprising is not that so many marriages failed or that so many women sooner or later fell apart, but that so many women tried so hard and recovered so well, that so many marriages were still intact with the potential for survival, and that some had not simply survived but were flourishing. (Gochros, 1989: 256)

"WELCOME TO THE QUEER BEDROOM": WOMEN BORDER DWELLERS TELLING THEIR "OUTSIDE BELONGING" STORIES

By stepping into the lives of these women and their partners, listening to their voices, experiencing their traumas, blisses and negotiations with their partners, with families and with their children; watching them in their workplaces, within their communities, and responding to wider social attitudes and silences, the diversity of these realities becomes apparent, challenging prevailing invisibilities, assumptions and stereotypes about love, sexuality, marriage, and family.

a sort of overrun . . . *debordement* that spoils all those boundaries and divisions and forces us to extend the accredited concept, . . . [but] it still will have come as a shock, producing endless efforts to dam up, resist, rebuild the old partitions, to blame what could no longer be thought without confusion, to blame difference as wrongful confusion! (Derrida in Kamuf, 1991: 256-257)

By exploring the different types of relationships that are negotiated, and the different issues that arise for sexually and culturally diverse women and their bisexually active/gay-identifying male partners, we hope to raise awareness of the broader diversity of relationships, and thus encourage health services, women's services, and gay community services to incorporate multisexual relationships into their programs and policies in order to promote and foster the emotional, sexual and mental health and wellbeing of these women, their partners and their children. For as women tell us, partners in multi-sexual relationships must deal with the issue that the outside worlds, whether they be heterosexual or homosexual worlds, will rarely consider the relationship valid as it does not fit neatly into the prescribed dualism of heteronormative marriage or homosexual relationship.

Contraries meet and mate and I work best at the limits of all categories. (Trinh, 1991: 53)

As Buxton concludes, a "comprehensive view of the polarized gay-straight controversy is sorely needed" and the solutions will be found "between the extreme positions" of traditional monogamous exclusively heterosexual marriage and exclusively homosexual partnerships (1991: 275).

We conclude this article with a final narrative based on two interviews with Lilith. We journey with her into panopticonic and confining public spaces where heteronormative and gender dichotomous discourses work to "dam" and police "contraries"; and into the "debordement" of private spaces such as the "queer bedroom" where identities, sexualities and genders shift, become ambiguous, meet and mesh.

Lilith and Adam pass for a "nice straight young couple." They get smiled at by shopkeepers, stopped by tourists wanting to use them as a frontispiece to an Australian backdrop. Lilith remembers the day the old woman reading a newspaper at the inner Sydney bus-stop watched Lilith and Adam share a breakfast apple, kiss and hug, before going separate ways for work. The old woman then said to her, "It's so nice to see a decent young couple like yourself these days. He looks like such a lovely young man. There's so much evil in this world. I've just been reading this." She showed Lilith the article on bisexual men doing the beats, going to orgies, while their poor wives knew nothing until the day a doctor told them they had an STD or HIV. "There's just no self-control anymore," she added, pursing her thin lips. "Not like in my day. We weren't even allowed to talk about such things."

Lilith wanted to tell her. Tell her about the other realities that existed, had always existed, beyond and within and between the monoreality presented out there. But she didn't, and hated herself for it. This old woman seemed so relieved, so excited that there were wholesome young couples around, and what would it mean to have this image destroyed? And anyway, weren't she and Adam "wholesome?"

Lilith couldn't bear the thought of those aging disillusioned and furious eyes, also struggling with a lifelong desire to be allowed to know more, to be allowed to say more, boring into her back for the fifty-minute bus-ride.

How could she begin to talk to this woman, to the wider world out there, even to supposedly radical and yet so conservative gay and feminist community members who refused to acknowledge her reality? Ultimately, it was the "sex stuff" everyone seemed to have a problem with, . . . except she and Adam.

Who are they? No one seems to quite know what to call them. Where do they belong? Nowhere, everywhere and anywhere. He is so gay and yet not gay. She is straight and yet in loving him, in fucking him, in sharing girlie secrets and taking the same men to bed at the same time, is she a gay man, or a gay man-woman?

She recalls the first time she knew she wanted to fuck him but can't recall who she was at that moment. He was lying stomach down on a rock under an apple tree in the park. He was running a finger along the surface of the lake watching his image blur and clear, blur and clear. She was admiring his butt squeezed into blue jeans and as she did so, another feeling glided into her: "I want to, I need to feel him inside with my fingers, slide my cunt over his butt, use my vibrator to fuck him." She felt hot as she lowered herself onto him, and began to grind. He arched his head back. His fingers dropped into the water, creating ripples, blurring their reflections. He knew they had now entered another border together.

They went home, and she licked his man-pussy and fucked him, whoever she was, and he was fucked, as he was used to with men, but now he was not quite who he had been. It was like they had done this before, and like they had never done this before, and in the very doing, they were no longer who they had been but who they were they could not say. Where did their "woman" and "man" selves begin and end? Where did their heterosexuality, homosexuality and bisexuality begin and end?

And fucking together in this border-zone, they knew they were now all of their selves and none of them only or completely. They were something else as well.

For many women of diverse sexualities and ethnicities in relationships with bisexually active men, who have actively and agentically moved into the border-zone of "outside belonging," or found themselves to be in it and have decided it is where they want to be, their lives remain externally unnamed, or resisted, or decried as "wrongful confusion." The words of Anzaldua are often echoed by many women we spoke to: "Who me, confused? Only your labels split me" (Anzaldua, 1987: 205).

DEDICATIONS AND ACKNOWLEDGMENTS

Sara: I would like this article to be dedicated to my mother Susan Thomas who has given me a questioning mind and strength to speak out. She is truly the best mum in the world. To my daughter Ella whom I hope I can give some of what my mother has given me. And to my partner Mark who has been there through good and bad.
Maria: This article is for Alan Stafford, for his strength and gentleness, for his love, and for resisting those who wish to pin him into a classification.

This is also for Alice and Soulla, pioneering women now deceased who were there when I first began to ask the questions that were not meant to be asked.

And for all the strong and beautiful women participating in our research.

REFERENCES

Acker, Joan; Barry, Kate; and Esseveld, Joke. (1983). "Objectivity and Truth: Problems in Doing Feminist Research." Women's Studies International Forum 6(4): 423-435.

Alley, Jo (1995). "The Missing Half: Women Partners of Bisexual Men." Women's Health Service, South Eastern Sydney Area Health Service.

Anzaldua, Gloria (1987). BORDERLANDS/LA FRONTERA: THE NEW MESTIZA. San Francisco: Spinsters/Aunt Lute.

Aruna, V.K. (1994). "The Myth of One Closet." In S. Lim-Hing (Ed.). The Very Inside: An Anthology of Writing by Asian and Pacific Islander Lesbian and Bisexual Women. Toronto: SisterVision.

Bauman, Zygmunt (1990). "Modernity and Ambivalence." In M. Featherstone (Ed.). Global Culture: Nationalism, Globalisation and Modernity. London: Sage.

Bhabha, Homi K. (1990). "The Other Question: Difference, Discrimination and the Discourse of Colonialism." In R. Ferguson, M. Gever, M. T. Trinh, and C. West (Eds.). Out There: Marginalization and Contemporary Cultures. Cambridge, Massachusetts: MIT Press.

Boden, Deirdre (1990). "The World as it Happens: Ethnomethodology and Conversation Analysis." In G. Ritzer (Ed.). Frontiers of Social Theory: The New Syntheses. New York: Columbia University Press.

Brew, Angela (1998). "Moving Beyond Paradigm Boundaries." In J. Higgs (Ed.). Writing Qualitative Research. Sydney: Centre for Professional Education Advancement, University of Sydney and Hampden Press.

Butler, Judith (1993). Bodies That Matter: on the Discursive Limits of "Sex." New York: Routledge.

Buxton, Amity Pierce (1991). The Other Side of the Closet: The Coming Out Crisis For Straight Spouses. Santa Monica, California: IBS Press.

Buxton, Amity Pierce (2001). "Writing Our Own Script: How Bisexual Men and Their Heterosexual Wives Maintain Their Marriages." In B. Beemyn & E. Steinman (Eds.). Bisexuality in the Lives of Men: Facts and Fictions. New York: Harrington Park Press.

Cohen, Ira J. (1987). "Structuration Theory and Social Praxis." In A. Giddens and J. H. Turner (Eds.). Social Theory Today. Oxford: Polity Press.

Connelly, F.M. and Clandinin, D.J. (1990). "Stories of experience and narrative inquiry." Teacher Education Quarterly 21(1): 145-158.

Davis, Stephen A. (1991). Future Sex. Armadale, Victoria: Awareness Through Education Publishing.

Denzin, N.K. (1997). Interpretative Ethnography: Ethnographic Practices for the 21st Century. London: Sage.

Derrida, Jacques (1976). Of Grammatology. Baltimore, MD: John Hopkins University Press.

Derrida, Jacques (1978). Writing and Difference. Chicago: University of Chicago Press.

Derrida, Jacques (1979). "Living On: Border Lines." In Bloom et al. Deconstruction and Criticism. New York: Seabury.

Derrida, Jacques (1981). Positions. Chicago: University of Chicago Press.

Dowsett, Gary (1997). Practising Desire: Homosexual Sex in the Era of AIDS. Stanford: Stanford University Press.

Epstein, Steven (1987). "Gay Politics, Ethnic Identity: The Limits of Social Constructionism." Socialist Review 17(3/4): 9-54.

Foucault, Michel (1977). Discipline and Punish: The Birth of the Prison. New York: Vintage Books.

Foucault, Michel (1978). The History of Sexuality (Volume One). New York: Pantheon.

Foucault, Michel (1984). "What is Enlightenment?" and "On the Genealogy of Ethics: An Overview of Work in Progress." In P. Rabinow (Ed.). The Foucault Reader. Harmondsworth: Peregrine.

Game, Ann and Metcalfe, Andrew (1996). Passionate Sociology. London: Sage Publications.

Giroux, Henry A. (1993). "Living Dangerously: Identity Politics and the New Cultural Racism: Towards a Critical Pedagogy of Representation." Cultural Studies 7(1): 1-27.

Gochros, Jean S. (1985). "Wives' Reactions to Learning that Their Husbands are Bisexual." Journal of Homosexuality 11 (1/2): 101-113.

Gochros, Jean Schaar (1989). When Husbands Come Out of the Closet. New York: Haworth Press.

Higgs, J. (ed.) (1997). Qualitative Research: Discourse on Methodologies. Sydney: Centre for Professional Education Advancement, University of Sydney and Hampden Press.

Hood, Daryl; Prestage, Garrett; Crawford, June; Sorrell, Tania; and O'Reilly, Chris (1994). Report on the Bisexual Activity/Non-Gay Attachment Research (Bangar) Project. National Centre in HIV Social Research, Macquarie Uni: Sydney.

Johnson, Sonia (1991). The Ship That Sailed into the Living Room. Estancia, New Mexico: Wildfire Books.

Joseph, Sue (1997). "She's My Wife, He's Just Sex." Sydney: Australian Centre for Independent Journalism, University of Technology.

Kamuf, Peggy (ed.) (1991). A Derrida Reader: Between the Blinds. New York: Harvester Wheatsheaf.

Kazmi, Yedullah (1993). "Panopticon: A World Order Through Education or Education's Encounter with the Other/Difference." Philosophy and Social Criticism 19(2): 195-213.

Lionnet, Francoise (1989). Autobiographical Voices: Race, Gender, Self-Portraiture. Ithaca: Cornell University Press.

Lubowitz, Sara (1995a). The Wife, the Husband, His Boyfriend . . . Her Story. Canberra: AIDS/Communicable Diseases Branch of the Commonwealth Department of Human Services and Health.

Lubowitz, Sara (1995b) "Women Partners of Bisexual Men." National AIDS Bulletin, 9(3): 38-39.

Lubowitz, Sara (1997). Three in a Marriage Video and Booklet Training Package for Health Care Workers. AIDS Council of NSW.

Lubowitz, Sara (1998). "Working with women whose male partners are homosexually active." At the 12th Annual World AIDS Conference, Geneva, June 28th-July 3rd, 1998.

Lugones, Maria (1994). "Purity, Impurity, and Separation." Signs: Journal of Women in Culture and Society 19(2): 458-479.

McGregor, Craig (1980). The Australian People. Sydney: Hodder & Stoughton.

McLaughlin and W.G. Tierney (eds.) (1993). Naming Silenced Lives: Personal Narratives and Processes of Educational Change. New York: Routledge.

Mason, Gail (1995). "(Out)Laws: Acts of Proscription in the Sexual Order." In M. Thornton (ed.). Public and Private-Feminist Legal Debates. London: Oxford University Press.

Molina, Maria Luisa "Papusa" (1994). "Fragmentations: Meditations on Separatism." Signs: Journal of Women in Culture and Society, 19(2): 449-457.

Nahas, Rebecca and Turley, Myra (1979). The New Couple: Women and Gay Men. New York: Seaview Books.

Pallotta-Chiarolli, Maria (1995a). "Choosing Not to Choose: Beyond Monogamy, Beyond Duality." In Kevin Lano and Claire Parry (Eds.). Breaking the Barriers to Desire: New Approaches to Multiple Relationships. London: Five Leaves Publication.

Pallotta-Chiarolli, Maria (1995b). "'Mestizis': The Multiple Marginalities of Living In/Between Social Groups." In Jan McNamee and Leonie Rowan (Eds.). Voices of a Margin: Speaking for Yourself. Rockhampton: University of Central Queensland Press.

Pallotta-Chiarolli, Maria (1995c). "'Rainbow in My Heart': Negotiating Sexuality and Ethnicity." In Carmel Guerra and Rob White (Eds.). Ethnic Minority Youth in Australia: Challenges And Myths. Hobart: National Clearinghouse on Youth Studies.

Pallotta-Chiarolli, Maria (1996). "Only Your Labels Split the Confusion: Of Impurity and Unclassifiability." Critical Inqueeries, 1(2): 97-118.

Pallotta-Chiarolli, Maria (1998). Cultural Diversity and Men Who Have Sex With Men: A Review of the Issues, Strategies And Resources. Monograph 3, National Centre in HIV Social Research, University of New South Wales; prepared for the Commonwealth Dept. of Health and Family Services.

Pallotta-Chiarolli, Maria (1999). Tapestry: Five Generations in an Italian Family. Milson's Point, Sydney: Random House.

Probyn, Elspeth (1996). Outside Belongings. New York: Routledge.

Rabinow, Paul (1984). The Foucault Reader. London: Penguin.

Richters, Juliet; Lubowitz, Sara; Bergin, Sarah; Prestage, Garrett; and Maurice, Robyn (1997). Women in Contact with the Gay and Lesbian Community: Sydney Women and Sexual Health Survey (SWASH 1996). Sydney: National Centre in HIV Social Research, Macquarie University.

Richters, Juliet; Bergin, Sarah; French, Judy; and Prestage, Garrett (1999). Women in Contact with the Gay and Lesbian Community: Sydney Women and Sexual Health Survey (SWASH 1998). Sydney: National Centre in HIV Social Research, Macquarie University.

Rubin, Gayle (1984). "Thinking Sex: Notes for a Radical Theory of the Politics of Sexuality." In C. S. Vance (Ed.). Pleasure and Danger: Exploring Female Sexuality. Boston: Routledge & Kegan Paul.

Rust, Paula C. (1992). "Who Are We and Where Do We Go from Here? Conceptualising Bisexuality." In E. R. Weise (Ed.). Closer to Home: Bisexuality and Feminism. Seattle: Seal Press.

Sewell, William H. (1992). "A Theory of Structure: Duality, Agency, and Transformation." American Journal of Sociology, 98(1):1-29.

Smart, Jeffrey (1994). "Coming In." Brother Sister. 22nd April: 9.

Trinh, Minh-Ha (1990). "Not You/Like You: Post-Colonial Women and the Interlocking Questions of Identity and Difference." In G. Anzaldua (Ed.). Making Faces, Making Soul/Haciendo Caras. San Francisco: Aunt Lute.

Trinh, T. Minh-ha (1991). When the Moon Waxes Red. New York: Routledge.

Weinberg, Martin S.; Williams, Colin J.; and Pryor, Douglas W. (1994). Dual Attraction: Understanding Bisexuality. New York: Oxford University Press.

Whitney, Catherine (1990). Uncommon Lives: Gay Men and Straight Women. New York: Plume.

The Lie with the Ounce of Truth:

Lillian Hellman's Bisexual Fantasies

Serena Anderlini-D'Onofrio

[Haworth co-indexing entry note]: "The Lie with the Ounce of Truth: Lillian Hellman's Bisexual Fantasies." Anderlini-D'Onofrio, Serena. Co-published simultaneously in *Journal of Bisexuality* (Harrington Park Press, an imprint of The Haworth Press, Inc.) Vol. 3, No. 1, 2003, pp. 87-114; and: *Women and Bisexuality: A Global Perspective* (ed: Serena Anderlini-D'Onofrio) Harrington Park Press, an imprint of The Haworth Press, Inc., 2003, pp. 87-114. Single or multiple copies of this article are available for a fee from The Haworth Document Delivery Service [1-800-HAWORTH, 9:00 a.m. - 5:00 p.m. (EST). E-mail address: docdelivery@haworthpress.com].

SUMMARY. This article focuses on the bisexual fantasies of play-wright and memoirist Lillian Hellman. It analyzes the 1934 Broadway success, *The Children's Hour*, and the short story "Julia," in her second memoir (1973), turned into a film in 1976. Both works are organized around a bisexual triangle of two women and one man, with one woman positioned as a bisexual, the other as a lesbian. The first is the autobiographical character, who understands her position as opportunistic yet chooses survival. The latter has a superior moral courage but succumbs to compulsory heterosexuality. Based on my theory of labial mimesis and dual female protagonists, I argue that the combination of Hellman's internalized biphobia and her repressed bisexuality was the psychological basis for her realism as a writer. The article also examines Hellman's difficulty in relating to real women, somewhat eased in transcultural situations where her guard against same-gender intimacy was down. The article is partly based in archival research in the author's private papers at the Harry Ransom Center Humanities Research Center in Austin, Texas. *[Article copies available for a fee from The Haworth Document Delivery Service: 1-800-HAWORTH. E-mail address: <docdelivery@haworthpress.com> Website: <http://www.HaworthPress.com> © 2003 by The Haworth Press, Inc. All rights reserved.]*

KEYWORDS. Bisexuality, fantasy, realism, polymorphous perversity, drama, memoir, Lillian Hellman, *The Children's Hour*, "Julia," *Pentimento*

INTRODUCTION

In 1973, at the height of her fame, the American playwright Lillian Hellman published a memoir, *Pentimento*, composed of stories focused on important people in her life.[1] She included the story of her friendship with one Julia, a playmate from childhood who awakened her erotic desire as an adolescent, and, eventually, lead her through an important anti-Nazi mission during World War II. Hellman never revealed Julia's identity. The chapter was then adapted to the film industry, and the film, *Julia*, was released in 1976. In the American media, the Julia story became highly controversial, with the author defamed as a liar and an ensuing libel suit that ended with Hellman's death in 1984.[2] In the past 16 years, little attention has been paid to Julia's powerful presence in Hellman's imagination, to Julia's role as a fantasy in her artistic development, and to the dire consequences of telling the Julia story for the writer's reputation.[3] I propose to view Julia as the life-writing trope that enables a positive bisexual interpretation of Hellman's first major play, *The Children's Hour*.

In today's lesbian, gay, bisexual, and transgendered communities, the word "queer" is used as an empowering category that aptly describes a variety of unconventional sexual and erotic practices that came under attack as a result of the AIDS crisis. The recuperation of this homophobic slur as a term of empowerment was a result of this crisis, and served the purpose of calling attention to the pervasiveness of non-normative sexual behaviors.[4] This process of self-empowerment destabilized categories of sexual identity such as heterosexual and homosexual, by pointing to the various ways in which the two intermingled and overlapped. In this article, I use the word queer in relation to bisexuality, which is viewed as specific subject-position within the larger, nondescript category. In the pre-Stonewall era of Hellman's time, bisexuality was a potential rather than an identity or practice. In Hellman it existed both as the fantasy to lie with a female and a male lover, and as her ability to be involved with more than one person at a time.

Hellman's sexuality was unconventional enough. She appears to have mostly preferred men, but was always nonmonogamous, both emotionally and sexually, and was known for preferring oral sex.[5] A divorcee whose primary partner, the older writer Dashiell Hammett, never quite divorced his wife (except in Mexico), Hellman was faced with the uncertainties of a legally unrecognized primary relationship. Her off-and-on companionship with her mentor lasted for thirty years, and became asexual in its ninth year.[6] It was punctuated by her flings with other lovers, and by the undertow of her passion for John Melby, a diplomat with whom she fell in love in Russia and whose proposal she eventually rejected.[7]

Her ethnic and racial identities were also hybrid. A second-generation American of Jewish parents who came from Germany, she lived at a time when her Jewishness was either constructed as an infamous racial inferiority, as in Nazism, or was passed as nondifference, as in the liberal democracies of the time, where a dangerous denial of eugenicism often operated.[8] Ironically, applying the postmodern category "queer" to Hellman evokes its previous homophobic and xenophobic uses. "Queers," like people from other countries, are often seen as "strange," "foreign," "uncustomary." They are made fun of and leered at. They learn to pass as a survival strategy. As a Jewish person who passed for a nondescript American most of her life, and as a heterosexual woman aware of her bisexual potential and latent homoerotic desires, Hellman was certainly aware of various passing modes.

In later life, she did admit to having occasionally consumed her homoerotic fantasies in her early years with Hammett. But these incidents happened in connection with alcohol and codependency on her male partner, and have reached us only through indirect testimonial evidence. In her sixties and seventies, Hellman had a relationship with the young writer Peter Feibleman. In his recollections, he reports her saying that even though Hammett "did not like homosexuality when he noticed it," there was a period in their love life when they "would get rowdy drunk together and sometimes take another woman home." When asked why this stopped, Hellman answered that she "got scared" of liking it.[9] In the process of writing her memoirs, Hellman accessed her suppressed bisexual feelings in conjunction with her effort to connect with her European roots as a descendent of German Jews. At that time, she came to experience what Adrienne Rich later named compulsory heterosexuality as a form of erotic totalitarianism.[10]

Throughout her career, Hellman strove to be a realist writer, one who started from her own experience and worked towards successfully hiding the process within the product. Having internalized the main phobias of her time, homophobia, bi-phobia, and anti-Semitism, she rendered them as key psychological motivations for her characters. The result was a series of widely popular dramas that honored the public's emotional intelligence and stimulated it. As a dramatist, she became an expert in lying naturally, while straddling between clandestinity and performance, the two registers allowed in the nonpluralistic, ideologically polarized societies of her time.

KILLING THE LESBIAN WITHIN: THE CHILDREN'S HOUR

A Broadway success of 1934-35, *The Children's Hour* was the first compassionate, albeit tragic representation of a female character in a lesbian position. It was Hellman's smashing debut as a playwright, and, as I claim, it is not coincidental that its author was a woman who was bisexual, at least in her fantasies. At center stage are the two female protagonists Martha and Karen. The first is positioned as a lesbian, for she has never been attracted to men in a sexual or romantic way, but admits to being attracted to Karen in such a way. Karen, who is attracted to her fiancé Joe, is positioned as a bisexual woman, for, after Martha's tragic death, she comes to some kind of reciprocation for her affection. The play's central trope is a slanderous lie that nonetheless causes the lesbian character to discover her unreciprocated love for her bisexual friend. The lie's resonance is amplified by the educational environment in which the play takes place, a boarding school for young women designed to acculturate them in their roles of wives and mothers rather than to free their creative intelligence and erotic imagination.[11]

Due to its subtle treatment of a sensitive theme that had been often sensationalized, this play enjoyed an unusually long and successful run of over two years. It was saluted as the "Thunderbolt of Broadway," and received mixed reviews based on what the critics of the time perceived as an ambiguity in defining the sexual orientation of the two female protagonists.[12] The author's ambivalence about lesbian desire, and that of the culture she was part of, are mirrored in the work's production history. Most commentators of the original production stressed the theme of the lie, thus focusing their attention on the adolescent Mary, the female student who fabricates it, in an almost "pure-evil," early-modern fashion.[13] Significantly, several reviewers refer to Mary as a latter-day Iago. Only later, the most sophisticated commentators of the time were able to analyze the denial of the unacknowledged truth revealed by her lie.[14]

The original production was quickly turned into a Hollywood film released in 1936, *These Three*. In accordance with the homophobic rules of the "celluloid closet" in effect at the time (Russo 1987), the film proceeded to heterosexualize the erotic energy that circulated among the three main characters. Instead of being accused of sleeping with Karen, Martha was accused of sleeping with Joe, Karen's fiancé, which made the plot a lot blander even though it retained some of the issues of trust between the two female characters. Hellman did not oppose this adaptation to the movie-industry production codes. She was the author of the screenplay for the direction of William Wyler (Wyler 1936). However, she felt uneasy about it for quite some time, and eventually became involved in the production of a film that restored the original plot and title, and was released in 1963. It starred Shirley MacLaine in the role of Martha and Audrey Hepburn in the role of Karen. This film went further than the play in emphasizing the long-standing interdependence and trust between Karen and Martha, and in analyzing the inner conflicts caused by their relationship and the way it was socially constructed. For example, the film expanded the story over a longer period of time, in accordance with the more relaxed style of the 1960s. It showed the two women as college mates, making decisions about their future together. At the end of the story, it also added a long sequence on

Karen, who is pensively walking in the park around the boarding school after her last words to Martha. As opposed to the play and the 1936 film, in this version Karen is not surprised by Martha's suicide, indeed, during her walk, she intuits Martha's intentions, and runs back too late to save her friend. Nor do we see her go back to Joe afterwards. This film was directed by William Wyler with the collaboration of Hellman (Wyler 1963). It is interesting that even at this time, she was opposed to characterizing both Martha and Karen as lesbians, even though, as Wyler's young daughter suggested, this seemed the most acceptable way to describe them with the public of the 1960s, and even though her resistance caused tensions in the collaborative effort.[15] Her rejection of a homosexual label for her characters can be read as an admixture of homophobia and a pre-discursive sense of bisexuality. It confirms that for Hellman desire was always multidirectional, and yet, due to the phobias she internalized, it would remain such only in potentiality.

The two female protagonists Karen and Martha form a labial duo, a figure of two-in-one at the center of the drama.[16] In the play's diegetic organization, this figure comes to symbolize the interdependence that characterizes female subjectivity and relationships.[17] The patriarchal order can only understand the two women's emotional and intellectual interdependence as "unnatural" for it bypasses the phallic symbols around which this order is organized. This is what causes the two to be constructed as lovers.

The text published in the 1970s, in the collected edition of Hellman's plays, presents two adult women who have chosen to be schoolteachers and are committed to their profession, even though one, Karen, also wants to marry. They maintain a certain distance from one another, and their personalities are not excessively outlined, either as opposite or as complementary. Other important characters are Mary and the group of girls with whom she interacts. She comes across as pushy and untrustworthy, clearly a spoiled child who will do anything to get her way. Also at the school is Martha's ageing aunt, Mrs. Mortar, who has been hired as a teacher probably out of a grudging kind of compassion, since she raised the orphaned Martha. Joe, the only important male character, is a physician. He is in and out of the school, since he spends quite a bit of his free time with Karen and the others. He is a nephew of Mary's grandmother, Mrs. Tilford, who has raised Mary and is very attached to her. The lie is what Mary invents to get away from the boarding school and from being punished for her negligence and for another lie. She runs away, and when home, to persuade her grandmother to let her stay, she claims that Martha and Karen's relationship is "unnatural." For the homophobic Mrs. Tilford, this obviously means that both women are lesbians and that they are lovers. Mary makes up this lie based on overheard remarks of Mrs. Mortar, who, just like any berating parental figure, blames Martha for being still single while Karen is engaged, and urges her to get a beau of her own instead of resenting her friend. But Mary has also been reading a novel by Théophile Gautier, which is circulating among the girls unbeknownst to all adults. *Mademoiselle de Maupin*, about a female bisexual transvestite who makes a living as a prostitute, is one of the best known representations of bisexuality in the 19th century, in the self-indulgent, hedonistic style that characterized the French fin-de-siècle. Inspired by this reading, Mary whispers in her grandmother's ears what she allegedly saw through the keyhole of Martha's bedroom.

As soon as Mary obtains her grandmother's permission to spend the night at home, Mrs. Tilford calls up the other mothers who quickly send for their daughters without an explanation. Karen and Martha bring Mrs. Tilford to court for slander, with Joe's support. But, since they have dismissed Mrs. Mortar, their main witness is not at hand, nor does she come back to testify. They are charged with "sinful sexual knowledge of one another" (55). When Mrs. Mortar returns, Martha attacks her and sends her away. Then Joe visits, and Karen interprets his reticence to touch her as proof that there is a doubt in the back of his mind. She sends him away, with a prayer not to come back for a while.

The play's recognition scene happens at this time. When the two women remain alone, Martha comes out to Karen and declares her love for her. She says, "I've loved you like a friend, the way thousands of women feel about other women," and insists that "it is perfectly natural that I should be fond you [Karen]." But when Karen replies, irritated, "Why are you saying all this to me?" Martha recognizes that her desire is sexual: "Because I love you . . . I love you that way . . . the way they said I loved you." A moment later, she concludes to a distracted Karen, "But I never knew it until all this happened" (62). Then Martha proceeds to position herself as a lesbian, by claiming that she "resented [Karen's] marriage," and "never loved a man" (63). Karen insists that she is "telling [herself] a lie." At that point, in the 1963 film version of the story, Martha asks "but why this lie?" "Can't you see" she insists with Karen, that this is "the lie with the ounce of truth?" (Wyler 1963). Yet in the play, the scene concludes with Karen's refusal to acknowledge Martha's confession. She does not accept her love for what it is, and this is what causes Martha to leave the stage and shoot herself in her bedroom.

As with Joe, Karen is indifferent to Martha, establishing herself as the survivor. The play represents the destructive wave of homophobia that causes her to "adjust" to heterosexuality, and the price she pays for this adjustment. When Karen loses the part of herself that is "lesbian" she also loses her best female friend, Martha. But immediately after the shot the reconciliation scene between Karen and Mrs. Tilford begins. Driven by an urge to tell Karen that she found out "it wasn't true," Mrs. Tilford arrives while Martha's body is still warm. She is too homophobic to know what the referent of this "it" might be. Is it Karen and Martha's sexual orientation or their sexual acts? Karen responds with a veiled irony, "You know *it wasn't* true?" (66, my emphasis). This indicates that Martha's suicide has "queered" Karen enough for her to know what the referent of that "it" might be. Indeed, Karen survives but is no longer sure that her sexual and affectional choices are right. In accordance with the homophobic conventions of the time, the play ends on a positive note for the straight viewer, when Mrs. Tilford encourages Karen to think about marrying Joe.

Yet in the body of the drama, Hellman emphasizes the moral integrity of the lesbian position, and the dilemmas of a bisexual woman's compromises. The play is inflected with the period's antifeminism and homophobia, but Hellman presented a female character who expresses her love for another woman, and this love is important enough for her to commit suicide. This is certainly a challenge to the phallocentric canon, wherein the traditional tragic female protagonist kills herself for a man, like Iokaste, Gertrude, Ophelia, Phedra and many others.

TRIANGULATIONS

While Martha is better described as a lesbian, Karen's character falls within the parameters by which bisexuals are typified in current psychological studies of sexual orientation, such as the Klein Scale.[18] Indeed, while both women display a social preference for women, Martha's preference for women also manifests as sexual desire and fantasy, while Karen's does not. Of course both characters have been co-opted in the paradigm that Adrienne Rich later described as "compulsory heterosexuality" (Rich 1980). They have never really been aware of alternatives to the institution of heterosexuality, and throughout the narrative they believe that it is best for a woman to enter matrimony under its terms. However, Martha eventually becomes aware of her sexual orientation, comes out to herself and declares her love to Karen. In the Darwinian logic of the play, Karen is a survivor fit for a heterosexist society who lacks the moral integrity of Martha. She loves women and is devoted to her female companion, but is "scared straight" by the circumstances.[19] Karen's ambiguity anticipates the tone of self-contempt that appears again in Hellman's memoirs.[20]

When she became a memoir writer, Hellman was known to the public as Hammett's lover and as his younger protégée who had eventually surpassed him and taken care of him in his later years. The presence of other current and former male lovers in her life was only known in her social circles. Despite the theme of her first major success, this might have suggested that she felt quite comfortable with her heterosexual identity. However, Hellman never became Hammett's official spouse. This made her vulnerable to the attacks of those inclined to construct her as a mistress or concubine who had somehow displaced a man's legitimate wife and mother of his children. Partly to offset this vulnerability, the memoirs tended to give center stage to Hellman's relationship with Hammett. Yet her unofficial status in the primary relationship of her life certainly brought her closer to the position of gay partners, whose long-time unions still go unrecognized.

She organized her second memoir, *Pentimento*, as a book of portraits of people in her life important enough to have functioned as a mirror for her own contradictory self. In the chapter "Julia," she destabilized her heterosexual identity even more radically than in *The Children's Hour* (*Three* 1979, 401-452). "Julia" utilized romantic friendship, adolescent homoeroticism, and other tropes typical of lesbian autobiography to foreshadow the higher awareness of her sexual and erotic desires that the adult narrator has gained from remembering the queering moments of her straight past, and from interpreting them as stations in a coming-out process. In Hellman's story, these moments are connected with the transculturalization process that destabilized the writer's national identity as a nondescript "American." This process presented her narrative voice in the effort to reach out for the specificities of her ethnic background and the Jewish and German roots of her ancestors.[21] By presenting Julia as an object of her homoerotic fantasies, and by placing her in the position of Martha, Hellman forged a "queer" sexual identity for herself. She also invented a transcultural partner who turned her back to the lures of success on the system's terms much earlier and more decisively than the writer ever did.

Julia's position within the Julia-Lillian-Dashiell triangle thus placed Hellman in the position of Karen. Admitting her own cowardice, the author refused to give her partner a full name and face, claiming fear of retaliation from her family, and of slandering her.[22] Curious readers were not satisfied, and Hellman was attacked as a forger whose recollections were made up. Eventually, she fell from the status of legend to that of a liar.[23] But in the framework of queer and bisexual studies, Julia can be reassessed as the fictional trope that allowed Hellman to express her bisexuality, and become connected with the queer aspects of her personality.

THE "LIE WITH THE OUNCE OF TRUTH": JULIA IN HELLMAN'S MEMOIRS

Hellman outlived Hammett and her own career in the theater by 23 years (1961-1984). She invented a second career as a memoirist partly as a result not feeling sufficiently recognized (Feibleman 1988, 34). In her four books of life-writing, she combined autobiography, memoir, portrait, fiction, and diary to offer a self-portrait whose authenticity has significance much beyond the literal truthfulness of the events narrated therein.[24] In the process of freeing herself from her dependence on Hammett and claiming full credit for her works, Hellman made an effort to soften up and display a more melodious and empathetic personality, and connect with her female identity and Jewish ancestry. In revealing more about her repressed bisexual fantasies, she reached for the parts of her own personality suppressed in her relationship with Hammett.

This effort is visible in the titles of two of her three memoirs. In *An Unfinished Woman*, the question of what is not finished remains unanswered, but one may speculate that it is Hellman's bisexual potential.[25] The title of the second memoir is an even more open admission of Hellman's regret about her decision to ignore her bisexual tendencies, "go straight," and benefit from Hammett's mentorship. An Italian word that means repentance, pentimento is used in English to refer to the "emergence of earlier images, forms or strokes that have been painted over and can be seen through an aged canvas."[26] Hellman explains that it refers to a painter's change of mind (1979, 309). In this book of portraits, pentimento bespeaks her regret that, in the past, her mask of toughness prevented a full awareness of other women's erotic and creative intelligence. Julia is her imaginary female mentor and object of erotic desire, whom Hellman made beautiful, intelligent, good, independently wealthy, and named after her mother. She also claimed to have risked her life for her in a clandestine anti-Nazi mission. When it became apparent that there was no evidence to confirm her recollection, the controversy started to rage.[27] Yet, Hellman's writings inevitably point to Julia's major role in her creative imagination.

In "Julia," Hellman revisited the bisexual triangle she had created in *The Children's Hour*, revealing the analogy between her own position and Karen's. The short story further positions the author as a realist writer who successfully hides the process within the product. Now a "legend in her own time" (Rollyson 1988, 1), Lillian confessed that as a young woman she knew about women's desire for each other and the powerful erotic energy it generates, but she embraced the safety of heterosexuality to survive. In the screen adaptation released in 1976, Vanessa Redgrave starred in the title role, Jane Fonda in Lillian's.[28] In an age of feminist activism for sexual and reproductive rights, the film presented two strong women of an earlier time whose friendship endured difficult trials. The bisexual triangle has an exceptional man on one side and an exceptional woman on the other. The Dashiell Hammett character (played by Jason Robards) is a retired successful novelist and screenplay writer, a one-time famed handsome gallant with an aura of radicalism his circle described as "the hottest thing in Hollywood" (Hellman 1979, 280). Julia is a female in control of a large fortune. Admitted to prestigious study programs like Medical School in Oxford and Freud's training in psychoanalysis in Vienna, she is now the leader of a large antifascist organization.

Lillian is the figure at the center of the triangle. She cannot embrace the univocal sexual identity that a monogamous relationship with either Julia or Dashiell would attribute to her. And she needs both mentors to become what she wants to be: a realist writer of drama committed to representing the experience of women in her day and age. She negotiates her position in the triangle by investing in a relationship with a woman who demands that she take political risks for her, while staying in a relationship with a man that protects her from the risk that this woman-to-woman affection be outed as sexual.

In the memoir, Hellman justifies her choice by showing how her female mentor Julia taught her how to lie naturally as she passed for an Aryan while smuggling Resistance money through the Nazi border. She is in a transcultural position, and as a bisexual, she can pass for a heterosexual by hiding the queer side of her personality. An assimilated second-generation American whose Jewish parents came from Germany, she is accessing her suppressed ethnic identity through her volunteer work in anti-Nazi resistance and solidarity. Bisexuality, or her sexual desire for Julia now sublimated as a desire to learn from her, is the secret

space of resistance to the regime of compulsory heterosexuality sym-
bolized by Nazi totalitarianism.

As a memoir story, "Julia" is a chapter that celebrates the romantic
friendship that inspired Julia and Lillian's commitment to end Fascism
and, by extension, intolerance and political tyranny. In the film Dashiell
is the constant lover in the background. Lillian travels to see Julia, and,
while traveling, she discovers within herself the nature of her love for
her. Thus, the memoir chapter can be regarded as Hellman's personal
"coming out" story, while the film is a more political and public statement about women's bisexual potential, and places her own bisexual
eros in the foreground.

Julia has rejected the glamorous lifestyle her background offered to
become a socialist. She knows that Fascism and Nazism eliminate diversity and its attendant right and respect. They cannot be combated directly because they are based on suppression and elimination. So she
operates an illegal antifascist organization situated near the Nazi headquarters, Berlin. Can the organization control the power of this political
hegemony without adopting its rhetoric? This is the question Julia can
answer for Lillian when she enlists her in a mission for the organization.
Julia's funds from her American estate are in Paris, in 1933 still the cap-
ital of a democratic state. Lillian is to carry them from the periphery of
the organization, to its center, in Berlin, where the headquarters of the
adversary are also located.

Julia is a distant mentor who withdraws herself. Yet from this distance she teaches Lillian to operate as an adversary of the totalizing system of subjectification established by Nazism and its allies. Hellman, a
realist writer, is committed to historical analysis, if not historical fact.
But she is unable to control her anger and so cannot lie naturally as a realist writer must do. Impersonated by Jane Fonda, Lillian is a Jew who
can pass for an Aryan and a prominent female traveling by herself. Her
grande-dame traveling style produces an aura of protection that travels
with her. As a neophyte, Lillian has to be gradually schooled into the
practice of interpreting the secret codes of a culture that lives under the
threat of totalitarianism. Without her knowledge, the organization
places the money she is carrying on top of her head, sown in the lining
of a stylish fur hat. She can wear it naturally because it becomes her
traveling style. So she learns to be natural in the persona constructed for
her by the architecture of the mission the organization has assigned to
her.

The student has been admitted to a work-study program in the organization. But she has to learn how to carry out the mission successfully

before she damages the organization and herself. When she begins to work, Lillian still has a univocal American consciousness: she believes that speaking out against injustice will make things right again. The American consciousness of her friend and mentor Julia has hybridized in the years of study in Oxford and Vienna. Julia knows that as long as she works for the organization, she cannot function in a direct way. Yet she has accepted the empirical evidence that clandestine organizations are the most effective in helping political dissenters to survive. Like Martha, Julia senses dangers before they arrive. She is aware of the threat Nazism posits to pluralistic societies, just like Martha intuits Mary's dangerousness in a phobic society. So Julia serves as a perfect mentor for Lillian. Flashback scenes show Julia and Lillian as teenagers in the US, when Julia taught Lillian directly. She read poetry to Lillian or led her in hiking trips in the mountains of her estate. Now Julia has changed method. She teaches Lillian through her organization, showing, at the same time, the perfection with which this organization operates, and the power she has to make it function and obey her.

Three moments of Lillian's trip show stages of her process of transculturalization in which she unlearns her univocal American identity to access her suppressed European and Jewish consciousness. They demonstrate the modes in which the transformation must occur and the power the leader of the organization has, a power she gradually confers to Lillian through her emissaries. They also show the sublimation into learning of the erotic energy that circulates between the two women.

With her friends, the two writers Dorothy Parker and Alan Campbell, Lillian is an American tourist in Paris enjoying the glamorous life Broadway and Hollywood success can buy. The first emissary, Mr. Johann is the only male collaborator sent by Julia. He is modest and dignified when he meets Lillian in the early morning, as she comes home from a night at a flamenco dance. He asks her to have breakfast at her expense, and controls her with the message from Julia he has given to the hotel concierge. When he sits with her in the Tuileries garden to explain the plan, he is courteous and explains that he has no time to be cordial. The two interlocutors speak from two different spaces of consciousnesses. Lillian has a scopic consciousness: she wants to see the matter clearly, and demands explanations before considering whether or not to commit herself. Like Karen, she does not know yet that there can be an ounce of truth in a lie. Johann knows that for the protection of the organization and herself, it is better for Lillian to know only what is necessary. Johann gives her the already arranged travel plans. Lillian's American consciousness is disturbed by what appears to be, and to a large extent is, a coercion, and she asks Johann to have a drink with her.

At this point the message Julia has sent serves to re-establish the communication between Johann and Lillian. Julia has reminded Lillian that she is often "afraid to be afraid." Julia refers to the fact that Lillian is called to participate in a serious operation. Her customary manner of pushing herself to be heroic, to demonstrate to herself that she is not afraid, could produce serious damage. Johann cannot get a commitment from Lillian, yet he knows that she might react according to what Julia knows about her. Therefore, he gives her the password for the next step: she is to meet him at the railway station at the train departing for Berlin at 6:00 PM, she is to say "hello" to him if she is ready, and pass him by if she is not. The first encounter with Julia's emissary shakes Lillian out of the glamorous complacency prompted by her American success, but the emissary leaves her when she is still uncertain. Does she want to learn what Julia knows already, and is she prepared to hybridize her consciousness? On a superficial appraisal, she looks like a very poorly qualified person for underground work: she is so foreign to the technique of lying naturally while conducting illegal work that she could quickly give away the whole organization. So one wonders why Julia wants to educate her, and what exactly Lillian hopes to learn from her, what power Lillian attributes to the secret of Julia's consciousness, and hopes to steal away as she accepts to work for her (Sargent 1990, 475-76). We can imagine a more empathetic Karen holding Martha in her arms when she confesses her love for her, and saving her from suicide with her desire to learn from her.

The second sequence analyzes an intermediate moment. Lillian has decided to accept, and is going to the railway station where Johann waits for her. Lillian wants to learn, yet she is barely aware of how conspicuously ignorant she is, of how much she has to learn. The sequence is complex. It begins when Lillian tries to evade the surveillance of her friends and is about to leave the hotel, when they see her and follow her in the taxicab to the railway station. Lillian is with two people who know her very well: Dorothy Parker, a member of her circle, is a fellow writer and a confidante; Alan Campbell, somewhat more distant from her, is accustomed to being her escort in the trips Dashiell declines to take. Lillian must not give away the reason for her changed plans, and must communicate the password to Johann, a person not of their circle, and unknown to her friends. Alan Campbell begins to suspect that Lillian is hiding something important. He presses her with questions about her former plans to visit her friend Julia in Vienna. Lillian diverts attention from Julia by claiming that she "never heard from her" (Sargent 1990, 479). But Alan notices that she is going to Moscow by way of Berlin, and warns her to protect herself. He says, "Lillian, you know what they do to Jews in Germany!" Johann advances towards Lillian in the railway bank next to the train. If she is not to accept the work, she is to simply "pass [him] by." And this is all she can do, besieged as she is by Alan's questions. When Johann is almost gone, Alan gives her the cues she latches on to get the plan to function again. Alan expresses his surprise at noticing that the person who is passing by them is the same person to whom Lillian was talking in the Tuileries garden. Lillian is clearly afraid that Alan has discovered the whole plan, but she calls Johann by name and gets him to turn back. Johann looks at her for a moment. He is perplexed. After all the useless and conspicuous noise Lillian and her friends have made, Johann has still not heard the password. But Lillian finally gets a hold of herself and says, "hello, Mr. Johann, I just wanted to say hello," in a loud emphatic tone (Zinnemann 1976, Tuileries scene; Sargent 1990, 470-80).

To smooth things out with her friends, Lillian introduces Johann to Dorothy and Alan, claiming to know that he came to the station to say good-bye to her. Johann denies that, and tells a lie containing the new password that will lead Lillian to the next step in the operation. He claims that he came to say hello to his nephew, Otto Franz, who is late, and asks Lillian to do that for him, in a specific place, "coach four, second class" (Sargent 1990, 480). Johann leaves as inconspicuously as he came along, having delivered his message. This is the sequence that shows Lillian at her most vulnerable moment. She has committed to resistance/queer work, denying her American/straight values of clarity and directness. Yet she still does not know what she is getting into. She also has to leave the familiar territory of her expatriate friends while she is still conspicuously and visibly American, and while she is directed to Germany where her Jewish background could be fatal to her. The visual text that gives images to this moment of Hellman's memoirs is most critical of Lillian's "Americanness" in that it almost cruelly indulges in showing her ineffectual glamour as a negative attribute next to Johann's modesty and effectiveness. The author is at her best in this moment in offering a critique of herself.

The voyage from Paris to Berlin is constructed as two series of sequences: one from the present in which Lillian sits in the train compartment with her hat on; and one from her memories of past moments in which her friendship with Julia developed. The young Julia was a lonely child like the young Lillian. Julia's racial traits correspond to the ones declared "superior" and truly Aryan by the Nazis: a pale, almost translucent complexion, blonde hair, and blue eyes. Lillian's colors are less diaphanous, and her eyes and hair are brown. Julia was from an old-money New England family and lived with her grandparents. It would seem that Lillian, a social inferior from a new-money family of Jewish Southerners, was the admitted friend Julia's grandparents welcomed as a sort of lady companion for their lonely granddaughter. The young Lillian admires the young Julia for her beauty and her learning, but it is not clear that Julia admires her. Lillian is also fascinated by the things Julia has, even though they do not make Julia happy and she begins to reject them at an early age. For instance, when Julia returns from the old continent, Lillian wants to know all about Paris and Rome, but Julia speaks to her of starving people in Cairo, and of how irate she was at her grandfather when he dismissed her urge to do something to help. Julia reports his indifferent "do not look at them" (Zinnemann 1976, second flashback scene; Sargent 1990, 493).

The episodes present moments during which the bond between the two young women grows. They happen in the bedroom, in a wood, on a boat, at a railway station, at Oxford, and in Vienna. The question of whether or not this is a sexual friendship is suspended, upstaging the issue of sexual identity to present the strength, durability, and range of the relationship it is based on. One reads these moments as ways in which the Lillian who is on the train interrogates herself on the mystery of why Julia trusted and continues to trust her. It would seem that Lillian is never sure of deserving the trust Julia posits in her.

The sequence of Lillian's arrival in Berlin presents the accomplishment of the learning process during the trip from Paris. Hellman's consciousness is now transformed. She has learned to think as a queer/transcultural person. The transformation is evident when she steps out of the train. The two main props of the operation are the fur hat in which the money is contained, and the candy box that has a distractive function for the police at the German border. In this scene Lillian invents a line in the script of the operation prompted by the candy box. On the train Lillian has had a younger and an older female escort. At her arrival a couple she does not know greets her by name, pretending to have seen her before. The younger escort prompts "give [the woman in the couple] the candy box." Lillian hands the candy box to the unknown woman naturally and improvises on the escort's suggestion "I brought you a present . . ." This encounter has the function of telling Lillian where to find her friend.[29]

In this scene Lillian's transformation, at least for what is necessary to bring the mission to completion, is accomplished. The female mentor who has instructed her is within walking distance of her, in a nearby café. The mere presence of this *mater-magistra* could inspire Lillian's creativeness in the last episode of the operation. But now that Lillian does not need any more lessons she can be a teacher instead. So, in this scene she functions as a vehicle for the "straight" American viewer to see the mechanisms by which totalizing systems of subjectification operate. The scene is almost didactic in the precision with which it presents the two registers of communication under which people operate. The official system uses the code of performance, the tone of voice is happy, complimentary, conventional, ceremonial. The unofficial system uses the illegal code, the tone of voice is low, it expresses no emotion, sentences are short, and serve to give operative instructions.

As soon as the greetings are over, the man in the couple takes Hellman's arm under his and tells her in a low voice where to find her friend. Then he greets her again in a complimentary, performative tone, and disappears in the crowd. So in a way what Hellman has learned is to function in two different registers as pre-Stonewall gay, lesbian, and bisexual communities always have. The first is a register of passing for a person accepting of and comfortable with the totalitarian system and the sexual identity it coerces. The second register is one of protecting the organizations in which resisting the totalizing system is still possible. In a totalizing system of subjectification the status of subjects of right which citizens have is eroded. Their identities are preserved in the unofficial systems of communication to which they must resort.

For Hellman, this means learning that a realist writer must operate in two different codes, one is performative, the other clandestine. Furthermore, it means learning that the secret of that "what" she needed to find to become a good student is the ability to entrust herself to a female mentor. Like a good realist writer, Hellman conceals the manufacture of her cultural product in the product itself. Therefore, neither the film nor the memoir answers the questions of who Julia is and whether or not she was Hellman's lover. But both film and memoir clearly indicate that, even in a patriarchal, heterosexist social order, it is necessary for women to learn from other women and not just from men.

The film version of the story focuses on Julia and Lillian's encounter in the café. Lillian delivers the money to Julia, and thereby becomes aware of her mutilation, suffered in the Vienna riots against German domination. Then Julia proceeds to tell Lillian about her little girl, named Lilly. Julia is a single mother and wants Lillian to take the child to America for protection. Both film and memoir versions conclude by narrating Julia's death as a Resistance agent, and Lillian's failed attempts to find Julia's daughter named after her. As in *The Children's Hour*, the Lillian Hellman character survives the totalitarian system that destroys her partner. And this new Karen is also unsure that her sexual and ethical choices are right.

REAL OTHER WOMEN

Hellman's relationships with women were more antagonistic than the example of Julia's story might indicate. In her social milieus, she was considered flirtatious with men and competitive with women, which in her time was typical of women connoted as hyper-sexual by their ethnic background, such as Italian and Jewish women. As a heterosexual player, she often flaunted her success with alluring guys, and, despite her flamboyant sexuality, she insisted on identifying as straight throughout her life. She rejected women's sexual attention, sometimes in significantly homophobic ways.[30] Hellman's allure was based on success and style, rather than looks, which for many people of her time was regarded in a woman as even more baffling. As a result, being friends with Hellman was not easy for women of her social milieus, nor did she always impact the lives of queer women around her in a positive way. In America, her closest female friend was Dorothy Parker, whose idiosyncratic and stormy personality matched hers.

However, Hellman did much better in transcultural situations and through her writer's aura. In their letters to Hellman, Raya Orlova and Helena Golisheva, her two Russain translators, display genuine affection and admirations for her. So do the women who wrote her fan letters about *Julia* and *The Children's Hour*. Hellman met Orlova during her first trip to Russia, in 1944, when she was saluted as a great playwright due to her ideology and style, which could pass for Socialist Realism. Orlova was with her when she visited the Leningrad front lines. This was a crucial time in Hellman's life, for she also met John Melby, the male lover with whom she had the most romantic story in her life. Golisheva is the interpreter she had during her second trip to Russia, in 1967, when she had just published her first memoir, *An Unfinished Woman*, and was coming back in fashion as a memoirist.

Both women were respected intellectuals of their time, and had their share of problems with the regime under which they operated. Hellman remained friends with them for the rest of her life. She often helped to ease their troubles and those of other dissenters recommended by them. Translators were respected in the literary milieus of which Orlova and Golisheva were part, since they were entrusted with bringing in ideas from more open societies. However, as female translators who were somehow constructed in this role by the gender system of their culture, Orlova and Golisheva might have transferred on Hellman their own aspirations to become writers in their own right. This made their relationship with her even more affectionate. Orlova's letters characterize her as a person of great spontaneity and deep emotion. Golisheva is more composed and ironic, with a more pronounced humorous side. Both are competent English writers, and their occasional use of unidiomatic expressions lends their prose a poignancy and elegance of its own.

The letters on both sides reveal an emotional intimacy and trust, which is not found elsewhere throughout Hellman's private papers. Both Orlova and Golisheva knew her from the practice of translating her works in another language. This gave them a strong sense of intimacy with the writer, which is manifest in their closing remarks. Expressions like "with much love," "don't forget me please," "yours very affectionately," "heartily," "yours with true love," "Lev [Orlova's husband] kisses your hands," "I miss you and would like very much to have a long talk with you," are just few examples of this emotional intimacy. The force of this emotional and intellectual interdependence comes fully across in Golisheva's comments about her own experience as a translator of Hellman. As she writes,

> how strange it is that I miss you . . . but I do, and I'm being sentimental of course, I knew you long before you knew me, because to translate a person is . . . to trace the underthought . . . It seems to me that I know the people I translate . . . better than their next of kin. And I like you–not only because I look like your grandmother![31]

Some of this epistolary intimacy might be a formality, yet Hellman accepted it and encouraged it throughout the friendship with the two women from Russia.

The numerous fan letters Hellman received in response to the two feminist staples of her career bear witness to the impact of *The Children's Hour* and *Julia* on lesbian and women's communities of their respective times, and to Hellman's many long-standing female would-be friends and admirers. Amongst the female fans of *The Children's Hour*, one claims to be Hellman's high-school mate and an early admirer of her talents.[32] Another supports Hellman's sympathetic approach to women's romantic involvements with one another, and offers criticism about her use of the word "dirty" in reference to Martha.[33] Still another is an activist in the gay and lesbian community of the time who congratulates Hellman on her treatment of homosexuality and invites her to contribute to funding a gay paper.[34]

The vast majority of letters for *Pentimento* are by female readers.[35] Many women of Hellman's age wrote to say that they recognized themselves in her life.[36] Younger women claim they found inspiration in her life.[37] Some were part of the Holocaust and wrote today that they found her account credible.[38] Finally, some women offered information on Julia and her child.[39] At least 30% of these writers refer to "Julia" as an empowering story that helped them feel prouder of their gender and more in control of their lives. Several writers specifically refer to the homoeroticism in the story as a source of self-empowerment. Others claim to be Julia or Julia's child.

Hellman's awareness of women's bisexual potential did have an impact on real women, both in the U.S. and abroad. Her fantasy relationship with Julia probably never materialized. But in transcultural situations she was capable of close bonds of emotional and intellectual intimacy with women. Many female readers were inspired by her works centered on women. They felt affinity for the situations they portrayed and empowered by the relationships between women she presented. In her imagination, a woman's bisexual potential was the ounce of truth that made univocal heterosexual identities a lie.

CONCLUSION

My discussion has focused on correspondences and parallelisms between the bisexual triangles in two excellent works, and on its author's ambivalent but productive relationships with women. Just like *The Children's Hour*, the Julia story is a "lie with the ounce of truth" that reveals its author's bisexual fantasies. Both stories can be productively categorized as "coming out" fictions in which the female character who occupies a bisexual position represents Hellman. They are realistic inasmuch as they present the lesbian position as untenable in a regime of compulsory heterosexuality. Both plots are set in the pre-Stonewall period, when queer sexual expression was repressed, and gay cultures were ghettoized. But the drama of the first labial duo is consumed at the same time that it is dramatized, while the second duo's narrative is remembered retroactively as befits a memoir's style. Therefore, "Julia" shows more of Hellman's introspective reflections on sexuality, and of her ability to think back about the subconscious motivations for her actions, including the decision to kill the lesbian figuration she had presented with Martha. Both fictions are based on a Darwinian logic according to which bisexuals, more than homosexuals, are fit to survive in a heterosexist society. Yet the realistic mode emphasizes Hellman's choice to focus on the moral dilemma of the female character in the bisexual position. Will she "go straight" and accept the law of compulsory heterosexuality, or risk annihilation by honoring the queer side of her personality? What effects is the death of her female partner going to have on her continuing life? And how are women in bisexual triangles to resolve their issues in biphobic and homophobic societies?

In a way, Hellman abided by the popular notion of her time that bisexuality is a field of pure potentiality, a capability to actualize Freud's proverbial "polymorphous perversity" whose energies, after the pre-Oedipal phase, are better redirected towards more socially acceptable and productive goals. This notion has been radically transformed by post-feminist, queer theories of bisexuality, such as those by Storr, Hutchins, and Kaahumanu, who focus on actual bisexual practices, and the identity-formation processes therein implied.[40] However, Hellman has the merit of foreshadowing patterns of interdependence between differently-positioned female queer subjects, and of presenting the circulation of queer erotic energy among humans independently of their awareness and/or acceptance of it. In both "Julia" and The Children's Hour the author denies the strong desire between the two female characters a sexual expression. But Lillian, the Hellman character in both film and memoir, is more sensitive than Karen. She truly admires Julia and is aware of her superior courage. Moreover, Julia dies as a hero rather than committing suicide. Yet in both stories the consciousness of the bisexual woman gradually hybridizes from a "straight" to a "queer" one, from one persuaded that there is only one sexuality, to one aware of the diversity of human erotic drives. This mirrors the gradual development of a bisexual identity and epistemology during the twentieth century, from the one that constructs its heterosexual component as a front that hides the queer side, to the one that proudly embraces bisexuality's multiple potential for love and for disrupting established binarisms.[41] In Hellman's case, the disruption of sexual binarisms spills over to other binarisms of her time, related to racism and nationalism.

In later life, Hellman mentioned the threesomes with Hammett and "another woman," but still felt uneasy about the lack of conventional romance in her writing style. As she told an interviewer, her writer friend

Dorothy Parker had rightly "pointed out to [her] that [she] had never, in [her] whole life, written a love scene" (Bryer 1986, 229). Ironically, Hellman did not count the wonderful love scene between Karen and Martha she wrote in *The Children's Hour*, and the one between Lilly and Julia in "Julia." This homophobic assessment of her own writing gives a measure of how difficult it was for her to come to terms with the bisexual energies that traversed her imagination. Her realism was marked by her own struggle to overcome her limitations, which endeared her to women in the public who identified with it. In the new perspectives opened by queer and transcultural studies, Hellman's bisexual fantasies can be connected with the triangulations of her plays and memoirs. This offers a better view of her subject position as both bisexual and transcultural.

Cabo Rojo, Puerto Rico, May 2002

AUTHOR NOTE

This article has greatly benefited from the documents available in The Lillian Hellman Collection, at the Harry Ransom Humanities Research Center (HRHRC), which I was able to consult thanks to a grant from the University of Austin, Texas. Pat Fox, Carol Henderson, Debra Armstrong, Elizabeth Richmond-Garza, and Tom Staley contributed vast amounts of energy to my project. I am especially grateful for their assistance during my stay.

NOTES

1. Hellman's second biographer, Carl Rollyson, calls her "A Legend in her Own Time" (1988, 1).

2. The four extant biographies of Hellman are by Mellen 1996, Newman 1989, Rollyson 1988, and Wright 1986. The most sensational accusation came from rival write Mary McCarthy, in 1980. It was leveled on television, during The Dick Cavett Show. McCarthy claimed that every word Hellman said was a lie, including "and" and "the." Hellman was watching the show and, against the advice of several friends and her lover Peter Feibleman, she decided to sue for libel. The suit ended with Hellman's death in 1984. The papers from this court action are in The Lillian Hellman Collection at HRHRC, Box 35, F-6. Biographers describe the ways in which the accusation of lying leveled against Hellman echoed throughout the media, with journalists and literary personalities investigating the truthfulness of her recollections, offering advice, and taking sides (Mellen 1996, 439-47; Rollyson 1988, 512-24).

3. Mellen interprets Julia as a psychological projection, and precisely as the person Hellman "would have liked to be . . . [one who] . . . did not need Hammett" (1996, 126). Tim Adams, a critic who focuses on the memoirs, agrees with Hellman's father that she "lived inside a question mark" (Adams 1990, 121-166).

4. Useful sources on this process are Lauren Berlant and Elizabeth Freeman (1993, 193-229), and Lisa Duggan (1992, 11-31).

5. Rollyson (1988, 67 and 74-106) on triangulations and ambiguous sexuality, Mellen (1996, 16 and 425-6) on oral sex and suggestions of a "lesbian past."

6. Hellman divorced her first and only husband Arthur Kober in 1932 (Rollyson 1988, 51). Her primary partner, Hammett, got a Mexican divorce from his wife Josephine Dolan in 1937. His daughters, and his former wife herself, never really accepted the fact (Mellen 1996, 127, 190, 344). Hellman and Hammett met in 1930 (Rollyson 1988, 41; Mellen 1996, 7). They stopped having sex in 1939 (Mellen 1996, 141). He died in 1961 (Mellen 339-49, 390-91; Rollyson 1988, 368, 385-93).

7. On Melby, see Mellen (1996, 231-37, 243-48, 258); Rollyson (1988, 222-46, 296-97, 344-45, 518); Newman (1989, passim); Hellman's diary of her 1944 trip to Russia, Box 110, F-5; Hellman's diary with notes on Melby and Hammett, when sick (1951 and 1960), Box 110, F-9; Hellman's letters to John Melby, Box 133, F-4 (HRHRC, The Lillian Hellman Collection).

8. Mellen points out Hellman's mixed feelings about her Jewishness, and her internalized anti-Semitism (1996, 31-2, 142, 167, 319, 423-4, 433). Her sense of inferiority with respect to whites of North-European, non-Jewish descent comes across forcefully also in an early version of "Julia" (Box 108, F-5). There, Hellman compares herself unfavorably to her friend Anne-Marie, a North-European type, due to her sweaty skin and lack of physical composure (1). She also describes the tall, lean, pale-skinned Hammett as a "very, very handsome man" (18), and Clare Boothe Luce as "a beauty," upon which Hammett replies that Boothe Luce's regular, unmarked features are all that "Jews care about" in appreciating a person's looks (18).

9. Feibleman (1988, 25); Mellen (1996, 40).

10. Adrienne Rich's argument was elaborated in the context of second-wave feminism (1980). She claims that, as long as men detain economic, institutional, and political power, it will be impossible to determine whether or not most women "choose" heterosexuality. Indeed, most women experience an autonomous eros when they breast-feed and when they embrace or care for each other. But, in many contexts, heterosexuality is still compulsory because women do not have the freedom to choose an alternative, either bisexual or homosexual. Rich implicitly subsumes bisexuality in the "lesbian continuum" on which women's relationships exist, even though, ironically, in the United States, a post-Stonewall lesbian cultural identity has defined itself in opposition to female bisexuality.

11. Hellman 1972, 1-70 (all quotations from the text refer to this edition).

12. N.A. "The Thunderbolt of Broadway." *Literary Digest*: 118: 22 (December 1, 1934): 20.

13. According to Brooks Atkinson, Mary was "diabolical." *The New York Times* (November 21, 1934): 23: 2. For Joseph Wood Krutch, her malice was comparable to Iago's. *The Nation* (December 5, 1934): 656-57. For Atkinson, who reviews again on November 29, she is a "pathological demon" who "almost throws the play off balance." *The New York Times*: D1, x:: 1: 1. For another reviewer, the script's theme is "double-headed." *Saturday Review*: 33 (March 2, 1935): N.P.

14. See reviews of the play's revival production in 1952. Richard Hayes. "*The Children's Hour*." *The Commonweal*: 62: 15 (January 16, 1953). Kermit Bloomgarden. "The Pause in the Day's Occupation." *Theater Arts*: 37: 5 (May 1953): 36.

15. The correspondence is in The Lillian Hellman Collection, Box 5, F-3, Items N. 1, 7, 8, 9, 10, 11, and 12 (HRHRC).

16. More on labial duos in my "The Figure of Two-in-One at the Center of the Dramatic Structure." In *The "Weak" Subject* (1998): 159-174.

17. This psychological theory, originally elaborated by Nancy Chodorow (1978), has been recently related to sexual and gender ambiguities by Lynne Layton (1998).

18. Udis Kessler explains the details and usage of this scale (1999). See also Klein (1985).

19. More about bisexuals being "scared straight" in Garber (1995, 512 & passim).

20. The British critic C.W.E. Bigsby refers to Hellman's self-deprecating attitude: "[In her memoirs, Hellman] reproves herself for a repeated failure to appreciate the value of her experience" (1982, 274).

21. A useful discussion of how differences other than sexual encroach on the process of life-writing can be found in Biddy Martin (1993, 274-93).

22. While the memoir was being published, Hellman's publisher sought legal advice on the treatment of her characters. The Julia story was flagged as a possible cause for libel, due to the negative characterization of Julia's parents and to the suggestion of sibling incest between two of the characters (HRHRC, The Lillian Hellman Collection, Box 31, F-6). Unfortunately, the writer's private papers do not provide any clear documentary evidence of her homoerotic friendships, and no woman is known to have claimed that she was her lover. Possible leads to the true object of the author's homoerotic fantasies are in the correspondence between Hellman and her two female interpreters in Russia, Raya Orlova and Helena Golisheva, and in the early drafts of her fourth and last memoir, *Maybe*. In both these sets of texts a woman named Frieda appears, and she could have been the object of Hellman's homoerotic fantasies (HRHRC, The Hellman Collection, Box 93, F-2 and Box 65, F-4, respectively)

23. The Julia controversy and the libel suit against Mary McCarthy were widely discussed by the press, in a number of informative articles. Cockburn 1985; Gelderman 1989; Glazer 1976; Kaus 1983; Mailer 1980; Mansfield 1983; McCracken 1984; McDowell 1983; McPherson 1984; Romano 1984.

24. The memoirs include *An Unfinished Woman* (1969), *Pentimento, a Book of Portraits* (1973), *Scoundrel Time* (1976) and *Maybe, a Story* (1980). The first three were republished with additions and a new foreword under the cumulative title *Three* (1979). Timothy Adams offers a quite perceptive literary analysis of them (1990, 121-166). He claims that there is authenticity in Hellman's autobiographical works, even though, obviously, as historical documents they are unreliable. He also points to the disclaimers Hellman places throughout them, and emphasizes the self-serving attitudes of her detractors.

25. The word unfinished has been variously interpreted. Some believe it refers to Hellman's testimony before the HCUA, some to her days in the theater, some to her personal relationships. Others believe it indicates modesty, the unassuming, self-deprecating attitude that characterized her voice. Others yet read it as an admission of her own untrustworthiness (Adams, 131).

26. *Random House Dictionary* 1987, 1435.

27. The controversy was further ignited by the publication of Muriel Gardiner's memoir, *Code Name Mary* (1983). Gardiner, who respected and admired Hellman, became aware of the similarity between her life and Julia's, and asked her about it in the letter dated October 26, 1976. Gardiner expresses the hope that Hellman will "[not] find this letter an intrusion" and specifies that "there is no need to answer it" (HRHRC, The Lillian Hellman Collection, Box 14, F-1). In closing, she reports one of the recent friends who called to ask her if she was Julia, had "cried himself to sleep after reading

[Hellman's] moving story" (Box 14, F-1). The two writers planned to meet but never got around to it, partly due to aging health conditions, and partly on account of the litigation anxieties that ensued (Box 14, F-1).

28. The Julia story appears in 1) the memoir chapter "Julia," in *Pentimento, (Three* 1979, 401-452*)*; 2) the film *Julia*, directed by Fred Zinnemann with the collaboration of Hellman (1976); and 3) the screenplay written by Alvin Sargent (1990). The screenplay is considerably expanded with respect to the short story. Some small discrepancies exist between the screenplay and the sound track of the actual film.

29. The wording of the screenplay is slightly different from the film: it says "I've brought you a small gift . . ." (Zinnemann 1976, Berlin railway station scene; Sargent 1990, 489).

30. An episode that displays Hellman's famously homophobic reactions can be found in her own introduction to the collection of her first three memoirs (*Three* 1979). In "On Reading Again" (3-9), she tells of how a wealthy woman whom she knew to be a lesbian made a minor pass at her in a taxi, after which she exited the vehicle in such a hurry that she fell on the street pavement and cut her knee. Hellman felt that her clumsiness was a result of her concern for not "hurting [the other woman's] feelings" (6). But of course, later on she realizes that the woman was more flattered by the effect of her pass on Hellman's behavior than hurt by her rejection. This indicates that Hellman was aware that other women's desire for her circulated in the energy filed around her regardless of how she identified.

31. The correspondence between Hellman and her two translators is in Box 93, F-2 (HRHRC, The Lillian Hellman Collection). The quoted letter is from the period after the end of Hellman's 1967 visit to the USSR.

32. Frances J. Ross (Dec. 28, 1934). All subsequently mentioned fan letters are in Box 6, F-3 (HRHRC, The Lillian Hellman Collection).

33. Mary Frank (Nov. 24, 1934).

34. Emma Sampson (N.D.)

35. These letters are in Box 6, F-3 (HRHRC, The Lillian Hellman Collection).

36. Janet Brown (N.D.); Peg Frankel (Oct. 7, 1973); Violet Fox (Sept. 23, 1973); Jean Grossi (Sept. 28, 1973); Janet Hess (July 30, 1973); Rita Knox (Jan. 16, 1974); Solita Solano (Sept. 29, 1973); Helen Stern (N.D.); and Katheryn Taylor (Nov. 28, 1973).

37. Ann Cook (Oct. 16, 1973); Marion Bell (N.D.); Richelle Jacobs (Jan. 4, 1974); Anne Laughlin (N.D.); Patricia Starr Hay (Oct. 24, 1973); Carol White (Oct. 1, 1973).

38. Henrietta Endore (Jan. 1st, 1974); Belinda Jeliffe (N.D.); and Myriam Portnoy (Sept. 11, 1973).

39. Mary Assheton-Smith (June 20, 1979); and Ellen Kailing (Oct. 8, 1980).

40. Amongst the theorists of post-feminist bisexuality, Merl Storr, Lani Kaahumanu and Loraine Hutchins emerge as the ones who have most significantly analyzed the difference between current notions of bisexuality and older ones. These differences are mainly a result of the cultural changes brought about by the feminist movement. Traditional bisexuality was predicated on a man's alleged right to cheat on his wife. It was, therefore, an eminently sexist practice. Post-feminist bisexuality is responsibly negotiated among partners, and thus implies equity and choices for female and male participants alike (Lani Kaahumanu and Loraine Hutchins 1991, xiii-xxvi; Merl Storr 1999, 1-13).

41. I refer to Merl Storr 1999, 3-4 (on binarisms an bisexuality's potential to disrupt them); and 8-10 (on current work on bisexuality as a mode if knowledge or epistemology).

WORKS CITED

Adams, Tim. *Telling Lies in Modern American Autobiography*. Chapel Hill and London: University of North Carolina Press, 1990.

Anderlini-D'Onofrio, Serena. *The "Weak" Subject: On Modernity, Eros, and Women's Playwriting*. London and Cranbury, N.J.: Associated University Presses, 1998.

Atkinson, Brook. "Review of *The Children's Hour*." *The New York Times* (November 21, 1934): 23:2.

_____. "Review of *The Children's Hour*." *The New York Times* (November 29, 1934): D1, x:: 1: 1.

Berlant, Lauren and Elizabeth Freeman. "Queer Nationality" (193-229). In Michael Warner (Ed.), *Fear of a Queer Planet*. University of Minnesota Press, 1993.

Bigsby, C. W. E. *Critical Introduction to Twentieth-Century American Drama, Vol. 1*. New York: Cambridge University Press, 1982.

Bloomgarden, Kermit. "The Pause in the Day's Occupation." *Theater Arts*: 37: 5 (May 1953): 36.

Bryer, Jackson (ed.). *Conversations with Lillian Hellman*. Jackson and London, University of Mississippi Press, 1986.

Chodorow, Nancy. *The Reproduction of Mothering*. Berkeley: University of California Press, 1978.

Cockburn, Alexander. "Beat The Devil." *The Nation* (February 23, 1985): 200-201.

Duggan, Lisa. "Making it Perfectly Queer." *Socialist Review*: 22 (1992): 11-31.

Feibleman, Peter. *Lilly: Reminiscences of Lillian Hellman*. New York: Morrow, 1988.

Garber. Marjorie. *Vice Versa: Bisexuality and the Eroticism of Everyday Life*. New York: Simon and Schuster, 1995.

Gardiner, Muriel. *Code Name Mary*. New Haven: Yale University Press, 1983.

Gelderman, Carol. "Including 'And' and 'The' " (332-342). *Mary McCarthy*. London: Sidgwick & Jackson, 1989.

Glazer, Nathan. "An Answer to Lillian Hellman." *Commentary* 61: 6 (June 1976): 36-39.

Hayes, Richard. "*The Children's Hour*." *The Commonweal*: 62: 15 (January 16, 1953): N.P.

Hellman, Lillian. *Maybe, a Story*. Boston: Little Brown, 1980.

_____. *The Collected Plays*. Boston: Little, Brown, 1972.

_____. *Three*. Boston: Little, Brown: 1979.

Kaahumanu Lani, and Loraine Hutchins. "Bicoastal Introduction" (xiii-xxvi). In *By Any Other Name*. Boston: Alyson, 1991.

Kaus, Robert M. "The Plaintiff's Hour." *Harper's*: 266 (March 1983): 14-18.

Klein, Fritz, B. Sepekoff, and T.J. Wolf. "Sexual Orientation: A Multi-variable Dynamic Process. *Journal of Homosexuality*: 11 (1985, 1-2): 35-49.

Krutch, Joseph Wood. "Review of *The Children's Hour*." *The Nation* (December 5, 1934): 656-57.

Layton, Lynne. *Who's That Girl? Who's That Boy? Clinical Practice Meets Postmodern Gender Theory*. Northvale, N.J. and London: Jason Aronson, 1998.

Mailer, Norman. "An Appeal to Lillian Hellman and Mary McCarthy." *The New York Times Book Review* (May 11, 1980): 3.

Mansfield, Stephanie. "Muriel Gardiner: Echoes of 'Julia'." *The Washington Post* (July 6, 1983): B1-B4.

Martin, Biddy. "Lesbian Identity and Autobiographical Difference(s)" 274-293. In Henry Abelove, Michele Aina Barale and David Halperin (Eds.), *The Lesbian and Gay Studies Reader*. New York: Routledge, 1993.

McCracken, Samuel. "'Julia' & Other Fictions by Lillian Hellman." *Commentary* (June 1984): 35-43.

McDowell, Edwin. "Publishing: New Memoir Stirs 'Julia' Controversy." *The New York Times* (April 29, 1983): C-30 (L) col 1-4.

McPherson, William. "Hellman vs. McCarthy–in the Matter of Truth." *Washington Post* (May 15, 1984): A15.

Mellen, Joan. *Hellman and Hammett: The Legendary Passion of Lillian Hellman and Dashiell Hammett*. New York: Harper and Collins, 1996.

Newman, Robert. *The Cold War Romance of Lillian Hellman and John Melby*. Chapel Hill & London: The University of North Carolina Press, 1989.

Random House Dictionary of the English Language, Second Edition, Unabridged. New York: Random House, 1987.

N.A. "Review of *The Children's Hour*." *Saturday Review*: xi: 33 (March 2, 1935): N.P.

Rich, Adrienne. "Compulsory Heterosexuality and Lesbian Existence" (631-659). In *Signs*: 5: 4 (Summer 1980).

Rollyson, Carl. *Lillian Hellman: Her Legend and Her Legacy*. New York: St. Martin's, 1988.

Romano, Lois. "Ruling Backs Hellman." *The Washington Post* (May 12, 1984): C1: 1.

Russo, Vito. *The Celluloid Closet: Homosexuality in the Movies*. New York: Harper & Row, 1987.

Sargent, Alvin. "Julia" (446-502). In Sam Thomas (Ed.), *Best American Screenplays 2*. New York: Crown, 1990.

Storr, Merl. "Editor's Introduction" (1-13). In *Bisexuality: A Critical Reader*. New York: Routledge, 1999.

N.A. "The Thunderbolt of Broadway." *Literary Digest*: 118: 22 (December 1, 1934): 20.

Titus, Mary. "Murdering the Lesbian Within: Lillian Hellman's *The Children's Hour*." In *Tulsa Studies in Women's Literature*: 10: 2 (Fall 1991): 215-232.

Udis-Kessler, Amanda. "Notes on the Kinsey Scale and Other Measures of Sexuality" (49-56). In Merl Storr (Ed.), *Bisexuality: A Critical Reader*. London: Routledge, 1999.

Wright, William. *Lillian Hellman: The Image, The Woman*. New York: Simon & Schuster, 1986.

Wyler, William (dir.). *The Children's Hour*. Screenplay by John Michael Haynes. MGM Productions, 1963.

_____. *These Three*. Screenplay by Lillian Hellman. Samuel Goldwyn Productions, 1936.

Zinnemann, Fred (dir.). *Julia*. Screenplay by Alvin Sargent. Twentieth Century Fox, 1976.

POEMS

Ingrid Ehrbar
Heidi Reyes

http://www.haworthpress.com/store/product.asp?sku=J159
© 2003 by The Haworth Press, Inc. All rights reserved.
10.1300/J159v03n01_07

[Haworth co-indexing entry note]: "Two Poems." Ehrbahr, Ingrid, and Heidi Reyes. Co-published simultaneously in *Journal of Bisexuality* (Harrington Park Press, an imprint of The Haworth Press, Inc.) Vol. 3, No. 1, 2003, pp. 115-117; and: *Women and Bisexuality: A Global Perspective* (ed: Serena Anderlini-D'Onofrio) Harrington Park Press, an imprint of The Haworth Press, Inc., 2003, pp. 115-117. Single or multiple copies of this article are available for a fee from The Haworth Document Delivery Service [1-800-HAWORTH, 9:00 a.m. - 5:00 p.m. (EST). E-mail address: docdelivery@haworthpress.com].

FUCKING CATEGORIES
by Ingrid Ehrbar

I don't fit your fucking categories
and, Baby, I never did.
I'm a tri-cultural bilingual
dyke identified bisexual with a
nonstandard gender step-half.

Your theories don't fit me
and I don't fit your theories
That's why you can't see me
why you have so much trouble
accepting my existence.

So expand your frame of reference
cause I don't fit your fucking categories
and Baby, I never will.
There's a whole wide world
you're missing that I'm not going to give up.

THE OTHER
by Heidi Reyes

I am the *other*.
I have always been that vague indefinite *other*.
I have had to explain this for as long as I remember.
At first, I didn't feel the need.
But from years of experience, I had to do it.
I had to create another box.
I had to create a space for myself that people could understand.
I am the *other* still, but at least I have explained it
so that they could understand.
At least, in the process, I've come to appreciate who I am, the *other*.

BI FILM-VIDEO WORLD
Aimee & Jaguar

Regina Reinhardt

http://www.haworthpress.com/store/product.asp?sku=J159
10.1300/J159v03n01_08

[Haworth co-indexing entry note]: "Bi Film-Video World: *Aimee & Jaguar*." Reinhardt, Regina. Co-published simultaneously in *Journal of Bisexuality* (Harrington Park Press, an imprint of The Haworth Press, Inc.) Vol. 3, No. 1, 2003, pp. 119-122; and: *Women and Bisexuality: A Global Perspective* (ed: Serena Anderlini-D'Onofrio) Harrington Park Press, an imprint of The Haworth Press, Inc., 2003, pp. 119-122. Single or multiple copies of this article are available for a fee from The Haworth Document Delivery Service [1-800-HAWORTH, 9:00 a.m. - 5:00 p.m. (EST). E-mail address: docdelivery@haworthpress.com].

AIMEE & JAGUAR, directed by Max Faerbenboeck, produced by Guenther Rohrbach and Hanno Huth for Senator Film Production AG, Berlin, 1998.

Screenplay by Max Faerbenboeck and Rona Munco, adapted from *Aimee & Jaguar, Eine Liebesgeschichte, Berlin 1943,* by Erica Fischer. Koeln: Kiepenheuer & Witsch, 1994.

Conditions under Nazi rule in Germany have been a favorite subject of film, television, and books for the last 60 years. The treatment of Jews, being forced to wear the yellow star of David, and of homosexuals, with the pink triangle, are familiar to most of us. But the plight of lesbians and bisexuals during this time is not a familiar topic. The film *Aimee and Jaguar* is based on a real love story between two women in Germany, one, Lilly Wust, is of German descent and bisexual, the other, Felice Schragenheim, is Jewish and lesbian. In 1942, both live in Berlin and are at opposite ends of the social scale. A German production directed by Max Faerbenboeck, who also wrote the screenplay together with Rona Munco, the film is adapted from the book by Erica Fischer. Overall, the screenplay follows the book very closely except that it creates more dramatic action for today's public. The film is shot in German with English subtitles. As a voice-over narrator, the director uses the character of Inge Wolf, the German baby sitter and helper to the Wust family. He frames the film's beginning and ending with the present, starting off with an older Lilly moving to a home for seniors where she meets Inge again, and ending with the two women reminiscing about their common past.

Lilly Wust is played by Juliane Koehler. She is the mother of four sons with a husband fighting at the Russian front, and lives the life of millions of German women; cooking, cleaning, and taking care of her children with an occasional male lover. She is oblivious to the plight of the Jews and the political opposition. She has earned the highest award given to mothers who bore male children for Hitler, The Mother's Bronze Cross, or "Das Mutterkreuz in Bronze," which will later save her life. She meets Felice Schragenheim through Inge, who unbeknownst to her is bisexual and Felice's lover. She enters into a world both frightening and fascinating. She feels strangely attracted to Felice and after Felice kisses her, falls deeply in love. She is unaware that Felice is Jewish and does not know that the lesbian/bisexual friends Felice brings to her house are Jewish. Felice calls Lilly "Aimee" and herself "Jaguar." The two women write love notes, poems, and a marriage contract to one another, totally ignoring the chaos around them as if it didn't exist.

During a home visit, Lilly's husband finds the two lovers asleep in bed, arms entwined. After a bitter confrontation Lilly asks him for a divorce. Felice tells Lilly that she is Jewish and that she works for the underground. The two women enter into an even tighter bond until, through the betrayal of neighbors, Felice is arrested by the Gestapo and sent to a Concentration camp. We are not served with the usual scenes of Nazi concentration camps to drive home the horror of these times, instead the director lets us glimpse at it in a riveting, brutal scene of Felice's arrest by the Gestapo.

Lilly is told by the Gestapo that the only reason she is not arrested for harboring a Jew and for an "un-natural sexual liaison" is because she has born four sons for Hitler. She never sees Felice again. Inge and Lilly meet again in a home for seniors long after the war, where Lilly confesses to her that she has had only one thought in the past fifty years, her time with Felice.

Felice is played by Maria Schrader, who delivers a daunting, haunting performance of a person who is able to live and function without fear or regard for the present and the future. Juliane Koehler, who plays Lilly, lets us experience a naive and intense character. On a historical note, in 1981, at 68, Elisabeth Wust was awarded the "Bundesverdienstkreutz am Bande" the highest honor the government of West Germany bestowed on "unsung heroes." It was for hiding four Jewish women in her apartment from 1942-1945, three of whom survived the Nazi regime.

Being born in Germany, with a bisexual orientation and married to a Jewish man, this film allows me to glimpse at my fate had I lived during that time. It was a chilling experience to see this film and yet, it made me feel fortunate to be living in today's world.

BI BOOKS

Lines of Flight:
A Review of
Identity Without Selfhood:
Simone De Beauvoir
and Bisexuality

Jo Eadie

[Haworth co-indexing entry note]: "Lines of Flight: A Review of *Identity Without Selfhood: Simone De Beauvoir and Bisexuality*." Eadie, Jo. Co-published simultaneously in *Journal of Bisexuality* (Harrington Park Press, an imprint of The Haworth Press, Inc.) Vol. 3, No. 1, 2003, pp. 123-132; and: *Women and Bisexuality: A Global Perspective* (ed: Serena Anderlini-D'Onofrio) Harrington Park Press, an imprint of The Haworth Press, Inc., 2003, pp. 123-132. Single or multiple copies of this article are available for a fee from The Haworth Document Delivery Service [1-800-HAWORTH, 9:00 a.m. - 5:00 p.m. (EST). E-mail address: docdelivery@haworthpress.com].

Identity Without Selfhood: Simone de Beauvoir and Bisexuality. By Mariam Fraser. Cambridge: Cambridge University Press, 1999. 215 pp.

If any recent text marks the coming of age of bisexuality as an academic subject, Mariam Fraser's *Identity Without Selfhood: Simone de Beauvoir and Bisexuality* may be the one. Less concerned with the need to justify its place or bring its readers up to speed than, say, *The Bisexual Imaginary* (Bi Academic Intervention, 1997); less convinced that the subject has never been tackled before than, say, *Vice Versa* (Garber, 1996) or *RePresenting Bisexualities* (Hall and Pramaggiore, 1996): Fraser's book assumes from the start that bisexuality is a key part of the contemporary cultural landscape–and treats readers as mature enough to know this. Finally, a book on bisexuality that feels as if it was written with the confidence that an informed and "bi-literate" audience already exists.

Fraser's aim is both to chart the ways in which Simone de Beauvoir's bisexuality has been variously constructed and erased by those who have written about her, and to put forward a larger theoretical account of the formation of modern identities and the possibilities for their re-working, rereading the French theorist Michel Foucault by way of his most supportive critics, the philosophers Gilles Deleuze and Felix Guattari. In its attention to detail, the book also marks a recognition of the legitimacy of bisexuality as an object of sustained academic en-quiry: the twists and turns taken by those who write on it, the different types of material produced by those who lived it. Best of all, she as-sumes that any given instance of bisexuality in culture–such as the re-ception of De Beauvoir–is infinitely rich and complex. Where Garber seems convinced that any given piece of bisexual culture can be wrapped up in a paragraph, Fraser feels that we have hardly begun to understand it. With each page the range of ways in which de Beauvoir's bisexuality has been invalidated are documented with greater precision, bearing witness to the right of bisexuality as a cultural phenomenon to be explored in depth. The accumulation of detail renders bisexuality an ever greater presence both in de Beauvoir's life and in the literature that has circulated around her. By the end it is clear that we cannot under-stand the reception of such a figure, unless we are willing to think long and hard about bisexuality.

Alongside her recuperation of de Beauvoir, Fraser proposes a sophis-ticated theoretical model that ascribes this evasion to more than simply some generic prejudice called "biphobia," but rather sees it as a product of a number of interconnected antipathies: to sexual experimentation, nonmonogamy, France, male-female relationships, existentialism, and feminism. At each point the opponents of that aspect of her life find it useful to evade or attack bisexuality, without bisexuality's necessarily being the particular object of hostility for individual writers. Rather, larger cultural concerns have converged conveniently to represent bisexuality as unnecessary to Simone de Beauvoir herself. These hostile practices operate by offering us constructions of a "plausible selfhood" (61): they claim to have identified a true or authentic de Beauvoir, given reality by an archive of photographs, diaries, and interviews with friends and lovers. They find in material such as de Beauvoir's expressions of guilt over her lesbian affairs "proofs" of her essential heterosexuality, as if every word or action were a revelatory key that contains an entire personality (Ch. 5).

But in each case Fraser wants to show how documentary archives produce a stability that de Beauvoir herself never exhibits. Her point is not simply that these accounts misrepresent de Beauvoir. Rather they misrecognize the nature of identity itself. For Fraser, identity is not organized around "durable properties" (98). Rather it is a set of "random events" (74), of inconsistencies or "lines of flight" that push in different directions. But identity faces a set of social processes that attempt to make us imagine ourselves as stable, unitary selves, contained by definitive terms: "I'm a depressive"; "I'm more attracted to women than men"; "I'm a poststructuralist." Any procedure that ascribes intent or a fixed "personality" may be seen to exemplify this process. According to Fraser, the claim that a discovered diary reveals its writer's true desire, or the claim that psychoanalysis can discern the unacknowledged motive behind an action is misleading–each of these "may be understood as one of the cultural formation which [prematurely] stabilize" the self (p. 59).

In each case, de Beauvoir's bisexuality is seen by those who write on her, and sometimes even named as such, but is never taken to be her true self. She is described either as a heterosexual woman with occasional lesbian dalliances, or as a lesbian manqué who was just born too early to embrace her true self. In another strategy, bisexuality is represented as being produced elsewhere: as a historical accident, which she would never have entertained had she not been on the Paris Left Bank of the 1960s; or as the atypical attribute of a distant philosophical star, which should never be entertained by us, her mere readers. A range of different discursive formations secures the absence of bisexuality, always seen as an epiphenomenon, which somehow attaches to the surface of de Beauvoir without constituting her core. Journalism frames it as a juicy scandal in a heterosexual marriage; the English frame it as a piece of risqué French exoticism. At each point, a different cultural group has its own distinctive reasons for needing not to acknowledge bisexuality.

Yet it remains unclear for whom this self is stabilized. Is Fraser documenting the way in which the *public image* of de Beauvoir has been rendered stable, or the way in which de Beauvoir's *own experience* of her self was made stable? It seems that it must be the former, since Fraser is careful never to claim to know de Beauvoir's own desires or to ascribe motives and intentions to her. De Beauvoir's own subjectivity *as she herself lived it* is never at issue in the book, but only "how the individuality ascribed to de Beauvoir is constructed" (164). Yet if it is only de Beauvoir's public image that is rendered stable, it is unclear how we should understand Fraser's concerns about "the high costs that processes of subjectification may incur" (165). Who is it who pays those costs? Presumably, at some stage these stabilizing forces press upon all of us, forcing us to reduce our possibilities. Yet it remains hard to know how we should measure the wider social effects of these stabilizing attempts. The archive that Fraser compiles suggests that certain sorts of consensus have indeed materialized around de Beauvoir, but how far have do these stabilizing effects reach? How accepting were the readers of the obituaries and the biographies? Does Fraser risk excluding the history of an active tradition of the radical affirmation of de Beauvoir's bisexuality? Deleuze and Guattari's position is that all our bodies constantly find ways to exceed the limits set on them by dominant notions of selfhood. Their work documents the ways in which lines of force exceed identity in our everyday practice. Of course, it is always risky to criticize an author for what might be the next stage in their larger intellectual project, but I am left wondering where, for Fraser, bisexuals *have* broken from selfhood in these ways.

One way of extending Fraser's work would be to look at how these dominant ascriptions of selfhood are changed when public figures are taken up as role-models. At a national bisexual conference in England, seminar rooms were temporarily renamed after prominent bisexual figures–with "The Simone de Beauvoir Room" occupying pride of place. Yet, following Fraser's suggestions we still need to ask to what extent this artificially stabilized model of a plausible self penetrates into our own constructions of our bisexualities. If the image of her that we receive has been stabilized, do we risk incorporating that stability ourselves? Or do we, as a community, have our own ways of understanding her bisexuality that exceed the conventions through which her life has typically been constructed?

This possibility of "excessive" understanding is a subject that Fraser seems reluctant to explore. For the most part, accounts of bisexuality appear only as examples of a failure to think bisexuality differently. While Fraser agrees with activists that bisexuality is disallowed as a legitimate self, she parts with them by arguing that to try to make bisexuality into such a self carries a terrible cost: it imposes rigid limits on the ways in which bisexuality can function as an identity (pp. 13-15). This parting of the ways with activist approaches to bisexual identity is a move which, I would suggest, is becoming a routine gesture at the more theoretical end of the academic bisexual discourse spectrum (one of which I myself am guilty–see Eadie, 1997).

In these gestures, the activist position is taken to be theoretically naïve, while the academic position is elevated as the more nuanced and insightful reading. Yet in practice, Fraser's trajectory has largely been prepared by the activist work from which she distances herself. The critique of the media's heterosexualization of bisexual figures; the challenge to lesbian feminism's rejection of male-female desire in its icons; the refusal to let the uncomfortable details of public figures be ironed out by academics who want to render their ideas without reference to their bisexuality: these are all approaches to the theorization of bisexuality begun in the work of activist campaigns. We need what Cooper (1995) calls a "generous" approach to activism, one which recognizes that strategies may have more productive consequences than our theoretical positions are able to recognize.

Ironically, Fraser is weakest at those points where she remains most wedded to key tenets in bisexual theory around which activists and academics have formed a problematic consensus. First, she clearly wants to retain a model of what we might call "bisexual exceptionalism": she holds that "bisexuality does not always author the self, or at least aspects of it, in the way that lesbian [sic] and heterosexuality are frequently perceived to do" (24). This dominant–and problematic– position within bisexual theory holds that bisexuality has a greater capacity to disrupt existing constructions of selfhood than other sexual identities. It is important to recognize, however, that this capacity is only a temporary one–only a production of the excessive ways in which, as Fraser shows, bisexuality has been made unthinkable.

We might want to say that this rendering of bisexuality as a logical impossibility has provided us with some leverage from which to challenge narrow beliefs about human sexuality, whose incoherence we are so well placed to reveal. That position makes sense–although we must then ask whether by stressing our disruptive potential we are supporting a strategy that mainstream biphobic culture needs: the representation of bisexuality as that which can never become a property of everyday life. More important, we must consider that the cultural logic of sexuality has changed dramatically in the twenty years since bisexuality made its latest comeback. Sexuality in general, and bisexuality in particular, has been repackaged as spectacularly visible entertainment, the ideal ingredient for talk shows, and even as a necessary fashion accessory for any modern identity. In the UK's recent version of the *Big Brother* TV show, for instance, no less than four of the ten contestants claimed to be bisexual at various points. The claim that we are assumed not to exist–or that we are in some way unthinkable–is firmly dependent on a particular historical configuration that no longer exists. For instance, to prove that bisexuality is more free from the assumptions of stable selfhood, Fraser cites the failure of writers to incorporate bisexuality into their pictures of de Beauvoir, how it always remains an uneasy, unresolved presence in writings about her. For Fraser, these examples show that "bisexuality is inarticulable in terms of the self" (123) and that "in the case of bisexuality, identity and selfhood are separated, such that they are no longer defined in terms of each other" (99). I would qualify both statements by insisting that what might have once been true–for particular writers in particular texts at particular times–does not enable us to generalize about bisexuality itself. These examples exist alongside very different ways of constructing bisexuality, all of which are historically changeable.

In Fraser's account, history is a troubling presence, and raises important questions about her methodology. Fraser is sceptical of those writers who attempt to explain de Beauvoir's identity with reference to historical limitations. Those who say that she could have chosen a lesbian identity had she been born later in the twentieth century, for instance, are rightly chastised for their projection back onto de Beauvoir of a particular position in lesbian political theory. And yet the question of history cannot simply be reduced to another strategy for stabilization of the self. The reluctance of writers on de Beauvoir to read her as bisexual is itself a historical phenomenon–and as bisexuality gains public visibility and academic legitimacy, it is inevitable that bisexuality will come to be seen as more of a presence in her life. As activists have sought to apply the term to, say, Oscar Wilde and Tallulah Bankhead, so the term has become one that writers on those figures increasingly use. "History" then is not only a rhetorical strategy used by critics, but also a necessary element in understanding why certain accounts of selfhood have become plausible, and how new accounts take their place.

Fraser's hostility to such historical readings is puzzling, since her own work tends very much in this direction. In asking how and why bisexuality has avoided becoming a solid type of selfhood, she is also, implicitly, asking under what conditions it might in fact become such a form of selfhood. We must surely read her work as a warning against the cultural processes in which we are currently enmeshed, which are solidifying bisexuality into just one more "authentic" self. For in the end, then, this account of bisexuality–as she herself makes quite clear–remains antithetical to a certain construction of "the bisexual self." To name de Beauvoir as bisexual becomes yet another type of "plausible selfhood," to be backed up with conventional types of evidence from diaries and letters, discerned in her decisions and disclosed by her actions. It can be reconstructed as the secret key to her philosophies and her politics, her emotions and her choices; and it will be only a matter of time (and of history) before we find ourselves reading titles like *Simone de Beauvoir: the Bisexual Philosopher.*

In this sense, Fraser's hopes may prove misplaced–and we surely need a historical perspective to indicate their limits. Rather than seeing bisexuality as necessarily less territorialized than homosexuality, I would suggest that like other sex-radical traditions, bisexuality comes in many forms: some are, as Fraser suggests, concerned with exceeding and subverting selfhood, but others are more firmly wedded to models of fixed identity. It may be that nascent sexual cultures are less caught up in the structures that regulate and distribute sexual identities and that, as one such subculture, bisexuality provides a good vantage point from which to unsettle assumptions about having "an" identity for desire. But unless we attend to the historical processes by which bisexuality is losing that potential, we cannot help but overestimate the extent of its ability to unsettle those categories.

Following on from this–and this is perhaps a problem with many Deleuzians–there are very real limits to the argument that bisexuality is valuable because it unsettles certain assumptions of stable selfhood and thereby proves that not all attributes can be made to cohere. From such a perspective, bisexuality finds its only value in rebellion: it's only good when it's bad. Such a position rules out entire areas of bisexual existence as too conformist–bisexual domesticity for instance. Jordan (1995:136-140) has pointed out that the attributes that Deleuze and Guattari validate are as likely to be practised by the police as by the revolutionary. Creative proliferation of lines of flight is not in itself politically progressive. Jordan's example is the swift and unexpected production of police road bocks in the English countryside to prevent raves. Equally, the rejection of territorialized identities is not inherently liberating–indeed, it is absolutely fundamental to the insatiable quests for consumption, which late capitalism most requires of us. In holding that bisexuality must always break away from norms, we are thus back with the dead-end of queer politics, where we prove our sexual credentials by claiming ever greater deviance, and thus become forced back into a new mode of authenticity: only the transgressive bisexuality is authentic.

This becomes particularly clear when Fraser reveals her own bisexual ideal through what she rejects. She is particularly scornful of the critics' attempts to make either men or women more significant than the other in de Beauvoir's life. She rejects both the accounts that claim de Beauvoir consorted women only to titillate Sartre and those that assert she merely loved Sartre because she had not yet discovered her authentic lesbian self. A positive bisexuality is held to be that which rejects and breaks out of this limiting view. Yet, this, in itself, narrows bisexuality by demanding that it never conform to these other possibilities. Is it possible to picture de Beauvoir as an actively bisexual woman, who was nevertheless often distant from the women with whom she had sexual relationships, in a way that she was not distant from Sartre? Is it possible to have a model of bisexuality that affirms the primacy of her relationship with this one man, while still affirming her bisexuality? Fraser seems to feel that any affirmation of Sartre's centrality in de Beauvoir's life must always be read as an attempt by critics to dilute her bisexuality. But what if her bisexuality was in fact constructed around the privileging of Sartre and the marginalizing of her sexual liaisons with women? Cagle (1996) has pointed out that bisexual politics has been drawn towards an account of bisexuality that is resolutely egalitarian in its desire to affirm bisexuals as equally committed to both sexes. Yet, driven partly by a desire to mollify our lesbian and gay comrades by assuring them that we will not–as they have always claimed–run back to our husbands and wives, we have sacrificed certain types of bisexual subjectivity: notably "trade men," precisely those who do go back to their wives after anonymous sexual encounters. Reflecting on this question, it has recently occurred to me that I value sexual relationships with women that last (and rarely enjoy those which are casual); and value sex with men that is casual (but seldom, if ever, enjoy that which lasts). Indeed, I may enjoy "casual" sex with men more than "committed" sex with women. It may even be more central to my sense of my sexuality in some ways–but it is not clear how well this can be articulated within a notion of bisexual gender egalitarianism.

De Beauvoir may pose just such a challenge. I do not claim to know how we would arbitrate between the assertions that de Beauvoir was powerfully influenced by the women with whom she had sexual relationships, and those, which state that they were minor diversions, undertaken often either to provoke or titillate Sartre. But we cannot simply assume that accounts that make her same-sex relationships subordinate to her opposite-sex ones are necessarily less true to her bisexuality. They may indeed be those accounts that best portray what bisexuality was to her.

I want to end by reaffirming my belief that this is a crucial book in the development of bisexual studies. I am motivated partly by my concern that I have spent some time detailing my disagreements. But this is because it has been some time since any work on bisexuality stimulated me to think so hard. Just as a generation of work was fuelled by the debates over whether or not the Klein Sexual Orientation Grid was a useful way of conceptualizing bisexuality, bisexual studies needs works like this that we can argue about. If there are places where my reading of bisexuality diverges from Fraser's, let these stand as lines of flight pushing out and away from this particular debate, and on towards a future bisexual studies, which, as Fraser reminds us so urgently, cannot afford to be shackled by any rigid sense of its own selfhood.

WORKS CITED

Bi Academic Intervention (Eds.) (1997). *The Bisexual Imaginary*. London: Cassell.

Marjorie Garber (1996). *Vice Versa: Bisexuality and the Eroticism of Everyday Life*. London: Hamish Hamilton.

Chris Cagle (1996). "Rough Trade: Sexual Taxonomy in Postwar America." In Donald Hall and Maria Pramaggiore (Eds.).

Davina Cooper (1995). *Power in Struggle: Feminism, Sexuality and the State*. Buckingham: Open University Press.

Jo Eadie (1997). "Living in the Past: *Savage Nights*. Bisexual Times." *The Journal of Gay, Lesbian and Bisexual Identity* 2(1): 7-26.

Donald Hall and Maria Pramaggiore (Eds.) (1996). *RePresenting Bisexualities: Subjects and Cultures of Fluid Desire*. New York and London: New York University Press.

Tim Jordan (1995). "Collective Bodies: Raving and the Politics of Gilles Deleuze and Felix Guattatri." *Body and Society* 1(1):125-144.

Index

ABIGALE (Association of Bisexuals,
    Gays and Lesbians), 38,41
Achmat, Zackie, 39
African countries
    bisexuality in, 44-50
    gay activism in, 36-39
    homophobia in, 35-38
    homosexuality explored in, 44-50
    lesbian and bisexual women in, 37
AIDS, bisexual men and, 3,40,57,
    63-64,67-68
Aimee & Jaguar (film), 121-22
Anderlini-D'Onofrio, Serena, 1-8,
    89-114
Anzaldúa, Gloria, 4,35,50
Apostles of civilized vice (Achmat), 39
appearance standards
    of bisexual women, 11-22
    effect of feminism on, 3,5,12-16,
        20-21
    effect of women's communities on,
        12,16-21
    heterosexual, 11
    lesbian, 11-12,16-17
    societal, 14,15
Arab culture, bisexuality in, 47-48
Ardener, Edwin, 48
Association of Bisexuals, Gays and
    Lesbians (ABIGALE), 38,41
Atwood, Margaret, 42
Ault, Amber, 45

Bankhead, Tallulah, 129
Beach, F.A., 47
beauty standards
    of bisexual women, 11-22

effect of feminism on, 3,5,12-16,
    20-21
effect of women's communities on,
    12,16-21
heterosexual, 11
lesbian, 11-12,16-17
societal, 14,15
Behind the mask (Website), 40
berdache, 29,43
Berman, K., 38
bi communities
    See also women's communities
    effect of, on beauty and appearance
        standards, 12,16-21
    weight acceptance in, 19-20
binary oppositions, 3,4,42-44,46-47,60
bisexuality
    in African countries, 44-50
    ambiguous nature of, 26,28-29
    in Arab culture, 47-48
    gender egalitarianism and, 131-132
    as an identity, 108,128-130
    interdisciplinary nature of, 8
    monogamy and, 30-31
    suppression of category of, 45-48
    transgressive, 130-131
"Bisexuality in the Arab world: An
    interview with Muhammed"
    (Gollain), 47
bisexuality movement, 3-4
bisexual men
    AIDS and, 3,40,57,63-64,67-68
    female partners of, 6
    labeled as gay, 41,46
    relationships with. *See* multisexual
        relationships
Bisexual resource guide (Ochs), 41

SPECIAL 25%-OFF DISCOUNT!

Order a copy of this book with this form or online at:
http://www.haworthpress.com/store/product.asp?sku=4871
Use Sale Code BOF25 in the online bookshop to receive 25% off!

Women and Bisexuality

A Global Perspective

___ in softbound at $14.96 (regularly $19.95) (ISBN: 1-56023-271-4)
___ in hardbound at $22.46 (regularly $29.95) (ISBN: 1-56023-270-6)

COST OF BOOKS _____

Outside USA/ Canada/
Mexico: Add 20% _____

POSTAGE & HANDLING _____
(US: $4.00 for first book & $1.50
for each additional book)
Outside US: $5.00 for first book
& $2.00 for each additional book)

SUBTOTAL _____

in Canada: add 7% GST _____

STATE TAX _____
(NY, OH, & MIN residents please
add appropriate local sales tax

FINAL TOTAL _____
(if paying in Canadian funds, convert
using the current exchange rate,
UNESCO coupons welcome)

❏ **BILL ME LATER:** ($5 service charge will be added)
(Bill-me option is good on US/Canada/
Mexico orders only; not good to jobbers,
wholesalers, or subscription agencies.)

❏ **Signature** _____

❏ **Payment Enclosed: $** _____

❏ **PLEASE CHARGE TO MY CREDIT CARD:**

❏ Visa ❏ MasterCard ❏ AmEx ❏ Discover
❏ Diner's Club ❏ Eurocard ❏ JCB

Account #_____

Exp Date _____

Signature_____
*(Prices in US dollars and subject to
change without notice.)*

PLEASE PRINT ALL INFORMATION OR ATTACH YOUR BUSINESS CARD

Name

Address

City   State/Province   Zip/Postal Code

Country

Tel   Fax

E-Mail

May we use your e-mail address for confirmations and other types of information? ❏Yes❏ No
We appreciate receiving your e-mail address. Haworth would like to e-mail special discount
offers to you, as a preferred customer. **We will never share, rent, or exchange your e-mail
address.** We regard such actions as an invasion of your privacy.

Order From Your Local Bookstore or Directly From
The Haworth Press, Inc.
10 Alice Street, Binghamton, New York 13904-1580 • USA
Call Our toll-free number (1-800-429-6784) / Outside US/Canada: (607) 722-5857
Fax: 1-800-895-0582 / Outside US/Canada: (607) 771-0012
E-Mail your order to us: Orders@haworthpress.com

Please Photocopy this form for your personal use.
www.HaworthPress.com

BOF03